STEP ASIDE

DAVID BRINDLEY

British and Foreign Bible Society
Stonehill Green, Westlea, Swindon, SN5 7DG, England

Cover Design by Jane Taylor
Printed and bound in Great Britain by Biddles Ltd, Guildford

CONTENTS

PREFACE

Leading residential Christian events is a challenge and a joy. For the last ten years I have been involved in organizing and leading such events for parishes, for those in training for various forms of Christian ministry, and for clergy. In this book, I have made no claims to originality. I have simply tried to pass on some of the experience I have gained during these years. Inevitably, my approach is magpie–like. I have picked up ideas and material from many sources, and from many people. I hope that I have acknowledged all these in the text.

My thanks are due to many people who have helped me to gain the experience on which this book is based. For the last five years the students of the Gloucester and Hereford School for Ministry have allowed me to experiment on them and try out ideas, and I am grateful to them. My wife, Gillian, and my three children, Matthew, Catherine and Rachel, have accepted that I have been away leading residential events on up to twelve occasions each year, and without their love and patience this work would not have been possible. I owe them more thanks that I can express.

I have tried to avoid the use of sexist language as far as possible, and rather than repeatedly writing he or she, etc., I have used the feminine pronoun in some passages, and the masculine in other passages. They are intended to be interchangeable.

STEPPING ASIDE

WHY GO AWAY?

Stepping aside from the relentless bustle of the world has always played an important part in the Christian life. John the Baptist and Jesus both spent time in the desert receiving strength from the Father for their ministries. Jesus regularly withdrew for prayer and re–assessment, and encouraged his disciples to do the same. "Let us go off by ourselves to some place where we will be alone and you can rest for a while." (Mark 6.31) It is not often recognized that Paul, after his Damascus Road experience, spent a considerable amount of time learning and praying before beginning his active missionary programme. (Galatians 1–2)

The practice of stepping aside has, for much of Christian history, been preserved by the monastic tradition, but the benefits of going away for a short time are now recognized by the whole Church. Throughout the country, and indeed in many other countries, there has been great growth in the numbers of Christian groups living together for a day, a weekend, or even for a longer period. There is a wide choice of accommodation available for any size group, and it is easy to find places suitable for six people, or for three hundred people.

Why has there been such an increase in the number of groups stepping aside? Here are some of the reasons why Christians go away:

- to receive new vision

- to put their everyday life into a new perspective

- to create group cohesion and fellowship

- to learn without distractions

- to give time to concentrated prayer and reflection

- for relaxation and refreshment

- to make decisions and plans under the guidance of the Spirit

- as a symbol that all time belongs to God

One of this century's greatest writers on spirituality, Evelyn Underhill, clearly sets out the necessity and the advantages of stepping aside from the ordinary routine to be with God.

"Our so–colled civilisation gets more and more complicated, more and more noisy. It is like one of those mills where the noise of the looms makes it impossible for the workers to hear each other speak. And if we go on at it long enough without a break we begin to think the looms are all that matter, and we are merely there to keep them going, and must not bother about anything else. In other words, I am sure there is a real danger that Christian spirituality in its deepest and loveliest reaches will be killed out by the pressure and demands of the social machines and even of the ecclesiastical machine. Man will get ever more utilitarian and this–worldly, and will wholly forget his true relation to God . . . Even religion tends to become more and more pragmatic, utilitarian; more and more active, and less and less inward; more and more a chain of doing, less and less of an attachment of being. And so by a curious paradox, as man's physical universe gets larger, his true horizon shrinks. He has become a slave of the clattering loom. He can't hear his own soul speak. Now those who control the modern factory . . . know what this means in the exhausting and impoverishing of human material, in nervous tension, apathy, unrest. So there is no good factory without its welfare department, its rest room, its opportunity for quiet. To withdraw the worker from the clatter and pressure is to increase the quantity and quality of the work. So I sometimes think retreats should be regarded as a bit of spiritual welfare work; quite essential to the organisation of the Church, and specially to the efficiency of its ministers." Evelyn Underhill, *Light of Christ,* Longman, Green and Co., 1944, p.28.

An effective time away for a group of people does not just "happen". It needs careful planning and organization, and it needs an understanding of the range of elements which make an event successful, together with some insight into how groups of people interact when they are living together. To ensure that your residential event is successful you should include a variety of types of activity in the programme. It is important to achieve a healthy balance which includes worship, learning, fellowship and relaxation.

One of the great joys of leading residential events is the freedom they offer for experimentation and innovation. People are free from the ordinary routine of home and occupation, and also free from the routine of Church life and worship. Try to capitalize on that freedom. Do not simply repeat what is done at home — take a risk.

SOME USEFUL ADDRESSES

There are a number of societies which aim to promote retreats. All can offer advice and support for those involved in this work.

The National Retreat Association, The National Retreat Centre, Liddon House, 24 South Audley Street, London, W1Y 5DL. This is an interdenominational organization, and publishes *The Vision,* which lists many of the retreats and conferences available throughout the country, and is a useful source of ideas. The Centre organizes training courses for retreat givers, as does the Association for Promoting Retreats, which can be contacted at the same address.

The National Retreat Movement, again at the same address as above, is a Roman Catholic organization, and can give details of many monastic communities which take guests, but do not appear in the main publications of addresses.

The Methodist Retreat Group, 34 Roslyn Avenue, Gedling, Nottingham, Notts., NG4 3NJ.

The Baptist Union Retreat Group, Baptist House, 129 Broadway, Didcot, Oxon, OX11 8RT.

United Reformed Church Silence and Retreat Group, 86 Tavistock Place, London, WC1H 9RT.

The following chapters aim to give guidance on how to organize a time away. Whatever the purpose of the event, there are many basic elements which remain constant. Such things as programme planning, dealing with bookings, and arranging worship, must be done well whether you are organizing a contemplative weekend for five people or an all–age activity week for fifty. The resources sections of this book (chapter 6–17) are taken from a wide variety of sources, and give some idea of the types of material which work in a residential setting. Most of the material included I have used myself, or have seen in use by others.

ORGANIZING A TIME AWAY

Organizing a weekend for forty people may seem a daunting task, but it can be made much simpler by careful planning. As you prepare for the time away, there are two parallel processes to work through. One is the task of working from a general purpose to a detailed programme (see Chapter 3); and the other, outlined in this chapter, is the practical organization which is needed to ensure that the event goes smoothly. At a number of points these overlap, and decisions made in one process will affect the other. Although it is helpful to describe them as two separate sets of tasks, you must ensure that there is adequate co–ordination between the two processes or disaster may occur. If the group organizing the worship want everyone joining in liturgical dance in the chapel, they need to know that the pews are screwed to the floor.

PRACTICAL ORGANIZATION

Where to go?

The purpose of your time away will, of course, have a bearing on where you go. Do you want peace and quiet, or would a town centre location be more appropriate for the event? Do you need to be close to any particular places or activities? How many people will be involved? What style of centre is required — the comfort of being waited on or the simplicity and involvement of washing up after meals? The timing of the programme will be affected if participants have to help with domestic duties. How much space is likely to be needed for large group activities? How many rooms will you want for small groups?

If possible, talk to someone who has experience of some of the retreat houses in the region. Personal knowledge is invaluable. When you have some idea of the size and style of the place you need, write for information. Most houses provide brochures or leaflets which give basic details, including cost, number of beds, etc.

There are two useful publications which give details of centres and houses in Britain. Both of them will give ideas about what is available in your area, and you may find out about some places which you did not know existed. Both are interdenominational, although they do indicate the denominational allegiance of the centres. *Away from it All: A guide to Retreat Houses and Centres for Spiritual Renewal* by Geoffrey Gerard is published by Lutterworth Press, and is revised every two or three years. Organized in regions, it gives travel directions, details about the number of rooms and other facilities, and a useful paragraph describing the style of each centre. Gerard has visited the majority of houses in the book, and his comments are valuable. *Out of This World* by George Target, (Bishopsgate Press, 1985) does a similar job, and contains photographs of many of the houses. Most of the centres, have not, however, been visited by Target, and he allows them to tell their own story. His book is aimed more at retreats than conferences, and he gives an interesting introduction describing different types of retreats.

Try to narrow down the choice to two or three places, and then visit them. A visit is essential — and it is important for more than one person to do this. Two or more pairs of eyes and ears can learn much from their different perspectives. It is also useful for at least one man and one woman to visit.

Visiting the house

When you visit, do not wander around aimlessly. Have a list of facilities you wish to see, and questions to ask. Most wardens are used to showing prospective guests around, and are happy to give advice about organizing events in the house. They are not, however, mindreaders. They will not know precisely what you need, so ask clear questions. You may find it useful to photocopy the following checklist, or to copy out the questions which apply to your group.

Arriving

As you are on your way to the house, be aware of how easy or difficult it is to find.

☐ Are the instructions provided adequate?

☐ What would it be like arriving in the dark?

☐ Is there sufficient car parking space?

☐ Is it well signposted?

☐ Is the entrance to the house obvious?

☐ Must cases be carried a long way?

☐ Take note of the outside. Is there a garden; are there seats?

☐ What sort of welcome do you receive? Does the place feel friendly and relaxed, or cold and dark?

The main rooms

Make careful notes as you are shown around the house.

☐ In the public rooms, how many people can be seated?

☐ Are there sufficient rooms for small groups?

☐ Can seating be rearranged?

☐ What audio visual facilities are there? Will you need an overhead projector, a video, a television, a screen, a flipchart, a photocopier?

☐ Is there a charge for using these facilities?

☐ Can soft drinks and snacks be purchased by guests?

☐ Is there a bar? Does it have set opening and closing times?

☐ Is there a library?

☐ Is there a room where people can go to be quiet?

☐ Is there a small room which can be used for one–to–one counselling?

☐ When is the front door locked?

☐ Are keys available?

☐ Is there a bookstall, and if so, is it well stocked?

☐ Are you able to suggest publications which might be of interest to your group?

Eating

- ☐ Is the dining room large enough for your group to sit in comfort?

- ☐ What is the system for serving meals?

- ☐ How long do meals usually take?

- ☐ Do guests help with serving; washing up; laying tables?

- ☐ What is a typical menu?

- ☐ Is there a choice available?

- ☐ Can the house cater for special diets — vegetarian, vegan, gluten free, low fat, etc.?

- ☐ Are meal times fixed, or can they be varied to fit your programme?

- ☐ Can packed lunches be provided if needed?

- ☐ If you are invited to do so, eat a meal!

Arrangements for worship

- ☐ Is the chapel appropriate for your group?

- ☐ Is there a piano or organ?

- ☐ What hymn books and service books are provided?

- ☐ Can the furniture be rearranged?

- ☐ Is there heating?

- ☐ Does the centre provide whatever you will need for celebrating the Eucharist?

- ☐ Are there periods when the chapel is not available, for example if the resident community has set office times?

Bedrooms

- ☐ How many bedrooms are there?
- ☐ Are there steep and difficult stairs; is there a lift; are there ground floor rooms for disabled or elderly people?
- ☐ Are the rooms all single, or will some people have to share?
- ☐ If there is more than one residential block, make sure you see a room in each.
- ☐ Are there washbasins; mirrors; adequate bedclothes; an easy chair; a table or desk for writing; somewhere for clothes?
- ☐ Inspect the showers and bathrooms.
- ☐ Are soap and towel provided, or must participants bring their own?
- ☐ Are there facilities for making tea and coffee when desired?
- ☐ Does the warden allocate names to rooms, or is that left to the organizers?

Relaxation

- ☐ What facilities are there for relaxation? Are there good walks in the area?
- ☐ Does the house provide maps?
- ☐ Are there games available for outside or inside?
- ☐ Is there a television? Are magazines, newspapers, novels, provided?
- ☐ Is there a shop or a pub nearby?

Business questions

- ☐ Is the warden resident, or is there another member of staff always on hand?
- ☐ What are the financial arrangements?
- ☐ When is a deposit required?
- ☐ When must you pay the remaining balance?
- ☐ What are the cancellation fees?
- ☐ Is there a discount for large groups?
- ☐ Are there any extra charges?
- ☐ How long in advance do you need to book?
- ☐ When does the warden need precise numbers, details of special diets, etc.?

The list may sound daunting, but not all the items will apply to every group. It is much better to make sure that you learn everything you need to know in one visit, rather than realize a few days before the event that you do not remember what hymn books are there, or cannot tell participants whether they must take a towel.

Booking

As soon as you have decided which house is best suited to your event, make the booking. It is a good idea to telephone first, with a selection of possible dates.

You will need to tell the warden:

- preferred dates

- arrival and departure times

- approximate numbers

- the nature of your event

- the age group of the participants

- the number of children (if any) in your group

- the name of the person who has overall responsibility

The warden will almost certainly require a deposit — probably of about ten percent of the likely cost, and will send you a form on which to confirm the details of the booking. When you have completed this, keep a copy.

If your group is small, find out whether you will be sharing the centre with another group? If this is likely, make sure that the events are compatible — if you are running a weekend of contemplative prayer, sharing with a youth group taking part in an all–night rock vigil could be difficult.

If you wish to change any of the details of the booking, let the warden know as soon as possible.

Costing the event

Now that you know the charges levied by the house you are going to, it should be possible to produce a rough idea of the costs involved. It is tempting simply to multiply the fees charged by the house by the number of likely participants in the event, but remember that there may be other costs, some of which may be quite significant. There is the price of leaders' accommodation in the house, assuming that they will not be paying their own costs. There may also be travelling expenses for leaders, and fees or perhaps a book token or similar gift for guest speakers. Estimate the amount which needs to be spent on materials — paper, pen, hire of videos, etc., and include this in your figures.

You should also take into consideration the cost of travel for the participants, which may add considerably to the total cost for the time away. If participants are paying for themselves, this can be daunting, especially for an event aimed at students or young families. Remember that the cost you estimate for a weekend may sound reasonable, but if most people need to add on transport costs it becomes less attractive.

Once you have a rough idea of costs, you should begin to draw up a budget for the event. Sometimes, the church or organization arranging the time away may be able to pay the whole cost, or may be able to subsidize the event to reduce the charge to individuals. Alternatively, those who attend will have to pay the full cost. In either case, it is important to produce a detailed budget so that individuals or the church can understand the level of financial commitment.

An initial budget might look something like this:

Accommodation

25 participants — house charges £50 for 48 hours	£1,250
2 leaders	£100
1 Consultant invited from outside	£ 50

Other costs

Consultant's travel expenses	£30
Book token or gift for guest speaker(s)	£30
Hire of videos	£20
Pens and paper	£30
Miscellaneous costs	£50

Total	**£1,560**

Divided between 25 participants is £62.40 each. The church is willing to subsidize each person by £20. The cost to individuals will, therefore, be £43.

Invite participants

The more notice you give of a residential event, the more likely it
is that you will attract a good number of participants. Ideally you
should publicize your event at least six months in advance. In
some cases you may want to publicize up to a year before the
event, particularly if you hope to attract people who you know are
busy. It is better to send individual notification to those you would
like to attend, or who you think might be interested rather than
relying on a general notice. At this stage a detailed programme is
not necessary, but you must give clear indication of the purpose of
the event, and a firm idea of the likely contents. You must also
give some idea of how much the event will cost. Is there a lower
price for shared rooms, or for children? If participants are unable
to afford the full cost, is there likely to be any financial help from
your church or any other organization? Including a small form on
which people can make a response, indicating likely interest, is
very helpful.

At some stage these indications of interest must be turned into
firm bookings. Perhaps three months before the event, write to
those who have returned the interest form, reminding them of the
dates and times, and giving them more details than appeared on
the original publicity. Ask them to return a form, together with a
deposit. On this they should show any particular dietary require-
ments.

Send a detailed programme to participants

About two weeks before the beginning of the time away, send a
detailed programme to those attending. This can be a simple duplicated piece of paper giving times and session titles, or for a large
event it may be a professionally printed booklet. It should contain
a map — most houses provide one which you can enclose or photocopy. There should also be details of things which should be
taken by participants — e.g. soap and towel, sleeping bag; pen and
paper; musical instruments; the results of any preparatory work.

Choose group leaders

It is possible to leave the choice of group leaders until you arrive at the centre. However, if you are planning a residential conference for more than about forty participants, or if you want those who will be leading groups to do some preparatory work it is essential to select people well in advance.

The leadership team will need to spend sometime drawing up a list of the qualities which are needed in the leaders and discussing other issues which may influence their choice. These might include:

- Experience in leading groups
- Sympathy with the aims of the conference
- A good balance of leaders (e.g. male and female, ordained and lay, older and younger, a range of church traditions, etc.)
- A sense of humour
- Good at timekeeping
- Relate well to a wide range of people
- Articulate, but not dominant

Invite the group leaders to a meeting well in advance of the event to brief them on what is expected, and to give them the opportunity to become part of the leadership team. If you envisage more than about a dozen groups, invite one or two extra leaders — it is likely that you will loose at least one through illness, bereavement, or for other reasons.

Give last minute details to the centre

As soon as the final programme is available, send a copy to the warden of the centre. It is probably acceptable to send final numbers at this stage, together with details of special diets. If any participants will not be present for the whole event, or will be absent for certain meals, inform the warden now — you will probably not be charged for meals missed if you give good notice.

Collect the money

You need to decide whether you will collect money as people arrive at the house, as they leave, or whether you prefer payment in advance. It is not satisfactory for people to approach you at odd times during the event with payment — it will inevitably lead to muddle. Be specific about when you will require payment, and to whom cheques should be payable — to the house, to the church, or to the organizer. It is not sensible for the money to be handled through a private bank account.

Hold a review meeting

After the event has finished and you have all returned home and had chance to reflect, gather together the leadership team to review the time away. Ask yourselves what went well in terms of planning, organization, content, relationships, etc. Then ask yourselves what went badly in each of these areas, or what needed improving. Present to the meeting a financial account of the event. You will find this is a very useful and important exercise for the leadership team, and it will be helpful if you plan another event in the future.

PLANNING THE PROGRAMME

Working from the initial idea that it would be good for a group of people to go away together for a few days to the detailed programme entails a number of steps. The first question to address is: who does the planning? There are many advantages in forming a group of perhaps four people to take responsibility for the event. The warden of one of the country's foremost retreat houses says that cancellations are most likely to be made when the minister attempts to plan and lead a residential session on his own without consulting any lay people. Within the group, it is sensible to give one person responsibility for the practical aspects of organization, and another the task of arranging worship. It is also helpful if at least one of the members has previous experience of running a residential event, or failing that, at least of being present at one. If the planning group becomes aware of some area of expertise which it needs but does not possess, then another member with the appropriate skills or experience should be recruited.

Refining the purpose

The first meeting of the planning group will concentrate on deciding on the purpose of the time away, and making some broad arrangements.

You may meet with a specific aim — the Church Council has decided to have a weekend to plan for a mission. Or the purpose may be vague — perhaps we should arrange a few days away for some people in the church to learn about different ways of praying.

How many people will be present? It is important to establish at the outset the most suitable number of participants for the event, this will determine many factors. Where to go, how to plan for work in small groups, the size of the leadership team, and many other things depend on the target number. If you plan a conference where it is likely that the group will be working together for most of the time, then twenty should probably be the absolute maximum. Above that number, there must be a large proportion of work in groups of no more than twelve. If the number of participants is likely to be very small, say under ten, you must try to ensure that there is sufficient variety of input — eight people can become stale with each other after a few days.

The leaders must begin by asking whether the stated purpose of the event is achievable, and how much time may be needed. A realistic goal is clearly essential — a conference or retreat which tries to deal with too many themes is starting at a great disadvantage.

So, at the initial meeting, after deciding the purpose, you will need to answer these questions:

- How many people will there be at the event?
- How much time do we need?
- Do we wish to invite outside speakers or consultants, or will sessions all be led by people from our own group?
- When should we go away?
- How will the time away be paid for?

Planning the process

Once the broad outlines of the event are decided, the planning group must begin to decide the process which it wants participants to go through. The questions to ask are:

- What point do we want to get to by the end of the event?
- What is our starting point?

Only when these two questions are answered will it be possible to plan the content in general, and then each session in particular.

You may have a firm idea of the point you want to reach by the end of the time away — you may, for example, need to present a set of firm plans to the Church Council. If you have some concrete aim such as this, it would be sensible to start with a wide brief, and successively narrow down as the event progresses. Working from the general idea of what Christian mission is for twentieth century secular society, through the needs of a particular community, to detailed proposals for your church would give a rough outline of how the planning group intend to approach the weekend.

On the other hand, you may have no such concrete plans for the event. Perhaps the aim is simply to spend time together in prayer and reflection, but there still needs to be some overall plan and sense of direction. A simple scheme such as looking at God's action in the past, considering God's activity in the present, and seeking God's guidance for the future will give participants a sense of movement through the time together and a map on which to locate their own thoughts and prayers.

Planning the content

Once the planning group has some idea of the starting point and the end point, and has made some decision about the length of time to event will last, then the detailed design of the programme can begin. Let the group brainstorm for up to half an hour on ideas for content, then eliminate those which do not seem to be strictly relevant. Put those which remain into a rough order. A group working on a programme for a residential planning a church mission might produce a list of topics like this:

An analysis of the state of Christianity in our neighbourhood.

What does our Church need to prepare for mission?

What does the Bible say about mission?

What experience does the Church in history have?

What prevents the Church from being missionary?

What resources do we have for mission?

Which groups in the community should we target?

What are the aims of evangelism?

Are we prepared for our church to change as a result of mission?

What does mission mean?

Are there different models of mission?

How can we welcome/teach/integrate those who come into the community as a result of mission?

Planning the sessions

When you have drawn up a list of possible topics, you should sort them into groups, and assign them to sessions in the residential event. In order to do this, you need to have in mind the number of working sessions you might have. Remember to have a sense of movement or progression running through the event. The above list of topics on mission could give rise to six sessions:

---

1. What is mission? — biblical and historical perspectives.

2. The state of Christianity in our Church and our neighbourhood.

3. Our resources for mission — what do we have and what do we need?

4. Models of mission we might use.

5. Training for mission — how do we prepare our Church to go out, and to receive new members?

6. Drawing up plans for action.

The next step in the planning is to ensure that a variety of different methods is used in the various sessions. The example of a conference to plan for mission gives ample scope for diversity. There is room for some direct input on mission in history and different models of mission, perhaps as a lecture or using video material. There could be group work — some Bible study on biblical models of mission. There might be a simulation game highlighting different methods of evangelism, and there could be small groups working on different aspects of planning for mission.

Recognizing that the mood of the group moves and changes during the residential event is an important element in programme planning. Chapter Four, *While you are there,* suggests some of the dynamics which may take place. A glance at this may help you decide what methods of learning are most appropriate at various times in the programme.

When appropriate methods have been decided, a leader should be assigned to each session, and given guidance about the styles to be used and the approximate range of content to be covered. It is good to use some variety of leadership during the event — one voice for a whole weekend soon becomes tedious. On the other hand, there should not be too many leaders — six different people might mean that the group never really settles.

Writing the programme

You now have the outline of the programme, with titles for each
session; some idea of methods to be used in each session, and the
person responsible for leading it. This can be put together with
times of meals to give the basic shape of the event. Do make sure
that you allow enough time for meals to be taken at a reasonable
speed. If people have to eat a meal quickly and bolt down scalding
coffee so that the next session can begin on time, they will not be
in a relaxed and receptive frame of mind. For forty people to eat a
meal, have a coffee, visit the bathroom, etc., will take longer than
you think. At least an hour is needed — probably more like 1½
hours.

The next step is to decide on times for worship and relaxation.
It may be decided to delegate details of worship to a small
sub–group, but they will need to be given some indication of what
is expected of them at various points in the programme. Does a
quiet, reflective form of worship fit best at a particular point in the
programme? Will time be allowed for participants to prepare for
experiment in worship? Chapter Twelve gives ideas about several
styles of worship.

Relaxation may be corporate or individual. Some free time is a
must — space for a walk, or even a sleep, will be needed by most
participants. And you must recognize that although the time away
is limited, better use will be made of it if members are relaxed and
refreshed.

All this work must then be translated into a written programme.
Even if it is only a list of times and titles on a single sheet of
paper, it is important that participants should have this in advance
— they will feel more secure about the event, and it will make it
more likely that they are ready to begin things on time.

Do consider the starting and finishing times of the whole residential event carefully. First, take travelling into account. Perhaps
the residential centre is situated in a place which is affected by
busy rush hour traffic, in which case arriving and leaving in the
early evening may be difficult and cause anxiety in people trying
to find their way around unfamiliar roads. If some of the participants are coming from considerable distances, ensure that they can
actually reach the centre for the beginning — it is very disruptive
if half the people turn up late. If some are travelling by train, check
the timetable to make sure that the journey can be undertaken in
the time available. Similarly, give thought to the finishing time. It

is tempting to squeeze as much as possible into the residential session, but it is not sensible to end late in the evening and expect people to drive long distances or to catch trains which will get them home in the early hours of the next morning — such things will inevitably lead to dissatisfaction, and probably to members arriving late and leaving early.

Secondly, consider when is a good time for the group to begin and end work. I have usually found that beginning at lunch time is not a good idea — most people are rather sluggish in the early afternoon, especially if they have eaten well. Experience suggests that starting at coffee time or tea time ensures that the group gels better — so if travelling times are a factor, arrivals at 3.30p.m., a cup of tea with a piece of cake at 4.00p.m., and beginning the first session at 4.30p.m. is a good plan. It seems that groups which begin with the evening meal come together most quickly, and if the event is a weekend residential this is almost inevitably the starting point.

Finishing times are not so critical, but thought must still be given to them. It is better to finish with lunch and then depart, rather than to try and work for one more session — the group will fizzle out after the meal, and everyone will be making plans for leaving. Ending with a meal also gives a good opportunity for participants to look back over the time together, and to say their informal goodbyes.

The result of those thoughts is that the best starting times are probably coffee, tea or supper, and the best ending times coffee or lunch, but that travelling constraints may mean choosing other, probably less ideal, times.

Some examples of what programmes might look like are given in the chapters which contains complete residential events (chapters 13–17). These are simple, but give a sense of direction and security to those taking part.

WHILE YOU ARE THERE

The most meticulous planning and the most exciting programme can be ruined unless you are able to manage the event well while it is in progress. The period of residence is hard work for those who are leading it — don't expect to be able to do anything else while you are there, and don't expect any rest — it will almost certainly be a sixteen–hour–a–day job.

PRACTICALITIES

Arriving

It is essential that at least one of the leaders should be at the centre ready to welcome participants as they arrive. Some will be feeling anxious and will need your presence and reassurance. Greet them, tell them which room they are in, and if possible take them to it. You should at least know in which direction the room lies. If you are collecting money at the beginning of the event, do so now. Make sure that you tick everyone on a list as they arrive — it may be needed for emergencies. If you are issuing name badges, have them ready at the welcoming point — preferably with participants' names already written on them. At small events badges are not essential, but if you have more than about twenty people who do not know one another well, they are a great help.

For very large events, it will be necessary to set up a proper reception area with tables and a number of people welcoming participants. It is a good idea to deal with names in sections of the alphabet at different tables — A to F at table 1, G to M at table 2, etc. Each of these welcomers will need to be fully briefed about exactly what is expected of them, and one of the leaders must be on hand to deal with any difficulties.

Be prepared for problems. I was helping to organize a large conference for over two hundred clergy in a University Hall of Residence. Everyone had been given a room number before arrival, and we had used the plan supplied to us by the University for this purpose. No–one had thought to mention to us that bathrooms and broom–cupboards also had numbers, so we had allocated two people to lavatories and two to cleaners' cupboards. Fortunately the porter was on hand to help sort things out.

As people arrive, make sure that they also know at what time the first event is, and where it is to take place. Some may wish to know where to find the public telephone, so they can assure their family that they have arrived safely.

However clear the instructions you gave on the programme were, someone will have forgotten something. Towels, soap and toothbrush are the most frequent. Usually a friendly word with the warden will produce the missing items to borrow or purchase.

Check the arrangement of the meeting rooms

Before the members of the group arrive, ensure that the furniture in the rooms is arranged as you want it. Nothing is less conducive to a relaxed start than the leaders rushing around moving chairs and tables as the first session begins. If you wish to make any drastic alterations, check with the warden. Check also that any equipment you have asked for is where you want it, and that it is working. For most events this will take about an hour. For a large event, however, you may need to arrive some hours in advance — once when I helped to arrange a conference for almost three hundred the leadership team were in position the day before the event started.

Make sure that the temperature of the rooms is pleasant. If it seems cold, ask the warden about heating arrangements. If it is likely to be stuffy — and it is surprising how quickly a room with forty people in it becomes airless — check that you can easily open some windows without too much disruption.

Notices

Good notices are important to the smooth running of the event. Not only do they help to make people feel secure, but they can prevent many things from going wrong. It is likely that the warden of the centre will want to welcome guests, and she may wish to run through the rules of the centre, such as arrangements for making beds, bookshop and bar opening times, their system for serving meals, the time the door is locked, etc.

Leader's notices should not be too long — often it will suffice to remind members of what they must bring to the next session, or of the time of the next meal.

Be available for counselling and direction

Almost any Christian residential event will stir up strong and unfamiliar feelings in some of the participants. Do not be alarmed if this happens — enabling people to explore at a deeper level than usual is after all one of the purposes of going away together. It is imperative that there should be someone available to help participants to explore and resolve these feelings. It may be that one of the leadership team is able and experienced enough to undertake this role. On a large retreat or conference it is often a good idea to invite someone to be around as counsellor or "chaplain" to the participants — the exact title will probably depend on the tradition with which the group identifies.

Do make it easy for group members to find the counsellor, and ensure that there is a place where confidential discussions can take place. It may be sufficient to announce that he will be available at certain times, or you may want to put up a list in a prominent place with times for participants to book. If you do this, it is enough for people to tick a time — some may be shy about signing their name.

Start and finish sessions on time

It is always tempting to allow a session to run on for a few more minutes, especially if it seems to be going well, but try to be firm — nothing will make you more unpopular with the house staff, particularly those in the kitchen, if you are regularly late for meals. Finishing promptly has the added advantage that it ensures that people are concise when making points. Starting on time is equally important — if you start punctually there is less need to run on late, and once you slide into the habit of beginning sessions five minutes late, it is very difficult to pull the group back from coffee for the advertized time.

Make friends with the people who matter

This applies first and foremost to those in the kitchen. If you quickly build up a relationship with the cook, you will find that nothing is too much trouble for her. If the meal is enjoyable, put your head around the kitchen door and say how much the group appreciated it.

Try also to make friends with the other staff in the centre — not only does it make the stay more pleasant for you, but it also means that if problems do occur then communication is so much easier.

If another group is using the house at the same time as you, make friends with its leaders. Ensure that you both understand which rooms each group is using, and how the groups are to be seated at meals. If the others wish to sit with members of their own group so they can continue discussion over meals, do not force them into matey conversations.

Leaders' meeting

It is essential during a long or large residential event to have a regular meeting of the leadership group to discuss progress and make adjustments and plans. On a conference of senior clergy from four Anglican dioceses which I helped to organize, the group of four leaders met together every time the participants were divided into discussion groups or workshops. This enabled us to keep our finger on the pulse, so that the next session could pick up issues which were being raised, and it gave us mutual support during the conference.

For some events, it will also be necessary to hold meetings of small group leaders during the time away. This is an especially good way of receiving feedback on how the programme is progressing, and it helps to ensure that the material or questions supplied are at an appropriate level. If there are more than about twelve group leaders, give one of the main leadership team the primary responsibility of relating to them, helping them with materials, etc. and chairing the meeting of group leaders.

Choosing groups

I have often seen a well–ordered collection of people descend into chaos when told to "Form yourselves into groups of six". A great deal of time can be wasted in this way. There are a number of reliable ways of allocating participants into groups, and the method used depends on the size of the groups, and how long they are to operate for.

For a brief, informal "buzz" on a topic, it is simple to ask people to turn around their chairs and talk to others in pairs, or in threes or fours. Above this number, however, and in the case of groups existing for more than ten or fifteen minutes, it is necessary to give more formal structure to the groups. For a large conference in which the groups will work together over a number of days, careful thought should be given to both size and membership. Ten to twelve is probably about the right size if they are to spend much time together — too small a number leads to staleness, too many means that some will not participate. If you are choosing the groups in advance, make sure there is a good balance in each — male and female, young and old, different Christian traditions, and geographical spread might all be relevant.

If you wish to split into groups while on the conference to discuss a list of questions, or to perform a certain task, going around the room and numbering everyone is the most reliable method. Start at an easily identifiable point in the room and then give people numbers in succession "one, two three . . ." up to the number of groups needed. This is better than designating blocks of six people, because it splits up friends. Then announce where each group is to meet — "All the ones in the sitting room; twos in the library," etc.

Tidy up afterwards

At the end of most conferences and retreats materials are left lying around and the furniture is out of place. One of the leaders should make a tour of the rooms which have been used when the event has finished, and take down anything stuck on the walls, throw away any rubbish left around, and put the furniture back as it was before you arrived. Not only is this a polite gesture to the staff of the centre, but you might want to come again!

HOW THE GROUP WORKS WHILE YOU ARE AWAY

The changing mood of the group

When any group of people live and work together, their changing and developing mood must be taken account of by those who are leading. Clearly each group is different, and the dynamic will depend at least in part upon the mix of personalities, but there do seem to be some guidelines which apply to most collections of people living together for a short period.

The movement of mood during a typical weekend might go like this:

Friday evening: Most people arrive expectant, but tired from the week's work. They are ready to be cooperative, but find long periods of concentration impossible, so avoid lectures. Some individuals may be feeling rather apprehensive, especially if they have not been on a residential event before, or if the house is unfamiliar to them.

Saturday morning: The group is fresh and interested. Most will be ready to work hard, and there is a positive sense of cooperation. This is usually a good time for direct input.

Saturday afternoon: The positive mood of the morning may well have evaporated, especially if some members are finding the pace difficult. If challenges to the leadership, or negative attitudes occur during the event, they are most likely at this time. Beware the session between tea and supper!

Saturday evening: The group is usually more reflective and mellow in this session. They cannot take much concentrated verbal input, but they are willing to pray, meditate, and often to share deep feelings and experiences.

Sunday morning: A sense of excitement is usually evident at breakfast on the final morning. Members are anticipating going home; they feel pleased with the time they have shared together; and they are preparing for the final act of worship.

One of the keys to working with a residential group of people is to recognize this movement of mood and feeling, and to work with it. Accept that at times the group will be positive and receptive, and at other times negative and resistant. Leaders should not blame themselves for these changes, nor should they fight against them. There is simply no point trying to give a group two hours of con-centrated talk after a good lunch on a summer afternoon. Effective leadership involves anticipating when shifts of mood are likely to take place, and incorporating them into the programme not as something to be fought against, but as another resource to be used.

Dynamics within the group

This is not the place for a lengthy description of group dynamics — introductory books on the subject are listed at the end of this chapter — but leaders need to be aware that most collections of people share some elements in the way they work. This is particularly true of residential groups, when the characteristics are heightened because they have more time to develop.

In any random collection of people, most of the following will be recognizable:

The "funny man". Laughter is an excellent way of breaking tension and of creating group identity, and leaders should ensure that it is present. Often, however, one member of the group sees his (and it almost always is a male!) role to entertain the others with a succession of funny stories and comments. In moderation, this is good, but it can get out of hand and can even become destructive if it turns to snide sarcasm.

The radical. Most members of Christian groups adopt a balanced position when discussing serious topics, but there is usually someone who tries to promote a much more extreme and radical position. One evening, after the "official" sessions had finished, a few people were discussing war. James held a pacifist position, arguing that fighting could never be right for someone following the Christian ethic. The discussion moved on to poverty, and he asserted that being Christian involved a St Francis–like attitude towards material goods. As the discussion progressed, he became even more insistent that pacifism and poverty were essential to the full Christian life. Next morning, James came to me during breakfast and, rather sheepishly, said that he felt he was being pushed into positions which were more extreme than be wished. This is a typical example of how someone who genuinely holds a fairly radical position becomes more definite as the time together progresses.

The ultra–conservative. This person is the opposite of the one described above. He or she sees the strength of the *status quo,* and as criticisms of it and suggestions for change develop, they will comment more loudly and aggressively that change for the sake of change is to be avoided. Often they are voicing the views of a small group who may not have the courage themselves to state their opinions. Like the Radical, the Ultra–Conservative should be listened to and taken seriously because he is probably stating what is being felt, but perhaps not articulated, by others.

The pessimist. "That's been tried before, and it didn't work". "We could never raise that amount of money". "They're all pagans in our area — they won't come near the Church". Many groups contain a person whose sole contributions are negative and pessimistic. It is necessary to have realistic members in a group, who do not permit the majority to get carried away on waves of unrealistic optimism. But too much negativity can be destructive.

The disrupter. The person who tries to sabotage the leader's plans is to be handled carefully. Sometimes he might be expressing the genuine feelings of a majority of the group that the tasks they are being asked to perform are inappropriate and should be changed or revised. Often, however, this person is someone who regularly wrecks group meetings by trying to impose his own interests and agenda on other people. Be firm!

The expert. This person has seen it all before and knows it all. He has a tendency to point out errors in what the leader says and does, and often refers to a retreat or conference he was at recently which was far superior to the present one and was led by a nationally known person. He probably drops names of important figures, and quotes from obscure books with impressive titles. He will often corner the leader after a session and ask lengthy, incomprehensible questions.

You can find most of the people described above in home–based Church Councils and discussion groups. There are, however, more opportunities for characters to appear when in residence, and these people will probably also be in evidence:

The loner. The person who sits by herself at mealtimes, who stands apart when drinking coffee, who goes for a lonely walk in the afternoon, and who rarely contributes to group activities, is not uncommon. It may be that she simply wants some time and space to herself, in which case the event is making an important contribution to her, and she should not be forced to be sociable. It is more likely, however that she finds social intercourse difficult, or that the surroundings are unfamiliar and she does not feel secure away from home. She may even be homesick. Try gently introducing this person to others, making sure that someone sits with her at meals. If the loner is severely isolated, it might be a good idea to ask some gentle person to look after her and make sure that she does not feel ignored or excluded.

The dominator. This person is forever trying to organize the others into complying with his own plans. He insists that certain people should sit together at meals; he organizes an expedition in the free afternoon; he makes sure that he wins all the arguments in the evening over coffee. In moderation, he can be a useful member of the group, for he ensures that everyone is included, but he can become tedious before long.

The over–familiar. The person who hangs around the leaders, tries to become close to them, and generally "creeps" can be very annoying. Usually this person addresses all her remarks in group discussions to the leader, and often implies that many of the things happening are for the good of the others, but are not really needed by her. This may happen because the person feels that she does not relate to the other members of the group, or that they are beneath her. Try not to let this person monopolize you, but integrate her into the group by involving others in conversation between you and her.

Handling conflict

Christian groups are often ambiguous about conflict, feeling that it should not occur in people who try to live according to the gospel. Conflict is, however, a simple fact of life, and both Jesus and Paul recognized that it will almost inevitably be present in the Church. Residential periods give the time and space for conflict to develop more fully than in the normal week to week life of the congregation, and anything which has been bubbling under the surface for some time is likely to come to the fore, especially if the event is a long one.

I knew that a day of liturgical dance might well be a flash point for conflict. Many of the participants were apprehensive about the activity, and there were a number of nervous jokes about it in the preceding days. On the actual day the dance was scheduled, Gordon absented himself, saying that he was going to visit his age- ing father. Everyone else joined in with enthusiasm, mainly because of the excellent teacher we had, and we produced two pieces of dance which would be included in the eucharist. Gordon returned as we were doing the final rehearsal, and sat and watched. A number of people were uneasy about this, and Janet commented that she found it very difficult to do this while being watched, and would Gordon please join in. He left the room crossly. At this, everyone felt bad, and one or two members left to pacify Gordon. Janet left in tears. Gordon felt unable to join in the eucharist, and many of the others felt sad and angry — some with Gordon and some with Janet. It emerged that Gordon was feeling upset about his visit to his father. The episode led to a number of people talking to each other about the relationships within the group, and to a certain amount of healing and reconciliation, but it left some anger and a great deal of hurt.

It is possible to use such conflict as a means of learning. If that is to happen, it must be acknowledged that conflict has taken place, and it must be recognized that real hurt and anger have been caused. And groups must not expect that the outcome will be all sweetness and light just because they are all Christians — it is quite possible that there will be unresolved emotions. This can, however, be a source of growth and reconciliation. Coming to terms with the fact that members must continue to function and work while acknowledging the presence of the conflict is a necessary part of the development of any group.

Occasionally the conflict may become extreme. A member of the group may pack up and go home, or an issue may take over to such an extent that the group stops working. On one conference, which thankfully I was not involved in leading, some members objected to the volume of photocopied handouts being distributed, on the grounds that it was both expensive and destructive of the environment. The arguments over the paper took up almost the whole of one day of the conference. If possible, the leader should try to remain dispassionate, and help the group evaluate what is happening to it, but on occasions such as this a firm but polite insistence that the group should continue with its main business is probably the best way forward.

The following suggestions are taken from *Leading Groups: A training course* by Margaret Parker, (Epworth Press, 1987) The book is specifically on training group leaders, but most of the material is equally applicable for those leading retreats and conferences.

How to ruin a meeting in twenty–six easy lessons

1. Put the chairs in straight lines facing the front.

2. Have the room either too hot or too cold, or ideally too hot at the beginning and too cold at the end.

3. Have inadequate light and place visual aids where at least half the group cannot see them.

4. Either assume that everyone knows a great deal and expect a great deal from them or assume that no one knows anything and treat them as if stupid.

5. Let vocal members dominate always.

6. Never listen to what anyone else says, but just wait until you can get your next speech in.

7. Occasionally pounce on a quiet person with a difficult question.

8. Express horror if someone says something you do not agree with.

9. Allow members to put each other down with derogatory remarks, and set an example by doing the same yourself where possible.

10. Suppress immediately any suggestion of genuine personal feelings being expressed.

11. Encourage platitudes and cliches.

12. Suppress any suggestions that any action should be taken arising out of the discussion.

13. Let as many as want to come to the group, preferably more than fifteen as this avoids close contact between members and enables you to adopt the role of teacher. Avoid any suggestions of breaking into smaller groups for discussion.

14. Do not let yourself think about what is happening in the group but just bat on regardless.

15. Start late and let the meeting drag on after everyone wants to stop.

16. Keep looking at your watch and occasionally yawning. Always speak in a bored voice.

17. Do not allow participation from any but the most boring group members. Do all the readings yourself and always introduce, dominate and summarize every discussion.

18. Never permit members to address each other in the meeting. Channel any observations through you.

19. Never have any variety in presentation of meetings.

20. Allow and even encourage members to take sides and take up entrenched positions on any subject.

21. Ensure that nothing is ever satisfactorily completed.

22. Frown on any sign of humour.

23. Criticize in a loud voice the behaviour of any children present.

24. Ensure that the seating is as uncomfortable as possible.

25. Ensure that there is a telephone in the room and always engage in a long conversation when it rings.

26. Ensure that there are the maximum number of external distractions.

Books

There are a number of good basic introductions to the way groups work, and also some which set these ideas within a Christian context. The following are particularly useful in a residential setting, although most were written with non–residential meetings in mind:

Adult Religious Education: Theory to Practice by Gemma Brennan and Kevin Cronin (Mayhew McCrimmon, 1984). This is good on a variety of methods of adult education, and on how adults interact while learning. Using some of the ideas for methods would ensure that an event does not become boring.

Making Adult Disciples by Anton Baumohl (Scripture Union, 1984). This book considers the place of attitudes, values, emotions and behaviour in Christian adult learning.

To be a People of Hope: Adult Education, a Christian Perspective by A. Patrick Purnell, Collins. The aims of adult education in a Christian context, and the process which adults go through while learning, are examined. There are good questions for reflection and discussion.

Useful books written for the secular market include:

Games People Play by Eric Berne (Penguin, 1968).

The Psychology of Interpersonal Behaviour by Michael Argyle (Penguin, 1990). An excellent analysis of group behaviour, communications methods, and social skills.

Group Living — the application of group dynamics in residential settings by Tom Douglas (Tavistock, 1986). Aimed primarily at social workers, but one of the few books which considers the group in residence.

WHAT MIGHT GO WRONG?

The list of things which might go wrong during residential conferences and retreats is endless. Most problems are fairly minor, and with common sense can be put right speedily. Occasionally, however, even the best organized conferences hit a major snag. Having some awareness of the possible pitfalls can help organizers to avoid the problems, because the majority are due to failures in planning or administration. Things which go wrong generally fall into one of three categories — problems of accommodation, difficulties with the programme, and breakdowns in relationships.

Accommodation problems

Getting the dates wrong is probably the worst thing which may occur, and it does happen even in the best places. The look on the warden's face when you turn up with thirty people and he expects you next week can be a sight to savour. This may, of course, be a disaster from which no recovery is possible. There may be a chance that the place is empty and can fit you in, or can accommodate a few people if rooms are shared. You might be able, if not too far away, to send some people home to bed, and use rooms in the centre during the day. But if you turn up and are not expected, it is clear that your retreat will not start on the right note. Just thinking about such a disaster can send shivers along the spines of the most experienced leaders of residential events — even now I feel some relief when I turn up to lead an event and find that I am actually expected. Making sure that everything is written down should help to guard against this. It is not uncommon for someone to telephone a conference centre with an enquiry about a date, and at the end of the conversation the caller is under the impression that the date has been reserved for them, while the warden thinks it was an enquiry which will be confirmed. If you have booked the dates several months in advance, it is worth writing or making a telephone call a few weeks before the planned event to make sure you are still expected.

Mistakes about the exact number of beds and meals are much

more common. If you book rooms for 30 people six months in advance of the event, it would indeed be surprising if there were no changes to the number. Last–minute difficulties such as sickness do occur, and houses are aware of this. Some places may make a cancellation charge, especially if a large number drop out, and you do not let the warden know well in advance. It can be more problematic if you turn up with more people than you have booked — however friendly and willing the staff, they cannot produce beds out of thin air. Again, the best safeguard is having things in writing. Make sure that participants are asked to fill in a form to confirm that they will be present. Asking them to pay a deposit in advance makes it less likely that they will drop out without giving adequate notice. Complications are most likely to occur when many of the arrangements have been done verbally, and when people assume that you have booked them in, when you thought they had only been expressing a mild interest.

Problems over meals are usually easier to deal with. Most kitchens are used to providing one or two more or fewer meals — it cannot be emphasized enough that making friends with the cook is an essential part of leading. The odd person who has forgotten to put "vegetarian" on the form can usually be catered for — most centres have a range of vegetarian, vegan and low fat meals in the freezer. Try to be clear in your requests, and to let the kitchen know immediately of any changes in your needs.

It can be more problematic if the food simply is very bad. Although most residential centres provide basic but very good food, general expectations of catering are now higher, and school cabbage and rice pudding are less likely to be tolerated. If you are self–catering, the problem should be easily remedied, even if it means driving a few miles to stock up at the nearest supermarket. I remember a youth event at which the person organizing the food was a very enthusiastic medical student who had just been taught about the advantages of a high–fibre diet. She came armed with many large packets of bran, and a series of recipes which made good use of it. Bran in soups, meat loaves, biscuits, and everything else imaginable soon caused a near riot. If the house kitchen is providing poor food, there is probably not much you can do about it — perhaps turning it into a running joke and organizing an illicit midnight feast might help, but be discreet in case the kitchen staff find out!

Programme problems

Perhaps it is best to begin with the worst possible problem again — the main speaker does not turn up. Or, almost as difficult, she informs you the day before the retreat that she is ill and unable to travel. This need not be such a disaster as it seems. If the event has been planned by a group of people who have carefully thought through the themes and programme of the time away, it should be possible for them to put together some relevant material in a short time, even if it involves staying up most of the night. If this happens, the participants will usually be very sympathetic, and will try hard to cooperate and make the event a success.

It may be even worse if the speaker does come, and turns out to be bad. In this case, it may be difficult to redeem the mistake. Firm suggestions that more time is spent in discussion groups, or that he allows more questions, may have some effect, but this might only be cosmetic. I remember a conference in which the speaker, a nationally acknowledged expert in his field was extremely boring. He read at length from a thesis he had written, and when the chairman indicated that the time to end the session had arrived, he carried on for another twenty minutes regardless. The one plus point was that the participants, rather than being annoyed, expressed sympathy for the organizers.

You should, if you are leading or speaking at an event, by aware of the possibility of having insufficient material. A talk you thought would last forty minutes ends after only fifteen; a game you had planned to take an hour lasts less than half that time, and it is clear from the mood of the group that they will not play it again. It is always a good idea to have some things up your sleeve — a video relating to your theme; one or two extra games; a short talk with discussion questions on a relevant topic; a series of Bible passages for groups to read and discuss. It is very little trouble to bring these along with you, and you might be thankful that you did!

It is quite common for audio visual equipment to malfunction. The overhead projector bulb blows; the video machine will not connect to the television, etc. You should certainly make sure these things work before beginning a session in which they are to be used, and it is a good idea to ask the warden where spare bulbs are kept. Many groups will have within them someone who is good with such machines — try to identify such a person at the beginning of the event. He will usually enjoy setting things up and making sure that they are serviceable.

Relationship problems

It is very rare that there are serious difficulties to do with the way people relate to one another on a Christian event. There may be stresses and strains, but these might be an inevitable part of a group of people living together for a few days. Perhaps the most disruptive thing that can happen is that a member of the group leaves in anger. I have only known this to happen twice — once due to a dispute over non–sexist language in worship, and once because a participant objected to playing "silly games". If a person is determined to leave, it is probably better not to try to stop them. Your efforts are likely to fail, and they will not feel comfortable at the event if they stay after threatening to take their leave. Do make sure that a member of the leadership team visits them after the event to try to resolve the issues. The group which has been deserted by one of its members is likely to feel hurt and confused, and you should have some discussion about the way the members have reacted to the person leaving.

The dramatic flare–up of someone leaving is rare. More often, there is some continuing anger or irritation. This may be resolvable — a group of people are talking too loudly late at night and keeping others awake. In this case it is simple to have a quiet and friendly word with the culprits — they probably had not realized that they were causing a disturbance. Sometimes extreme differences in views can cause conflict — the evangelical who thinks he needs to convert his catholic brethren, or the ritualist who insists on using incense in the worship to the annoyance of the evangelicals, can both be the catalyst for argument. It could be, however, that the source of irritation is less tangible, and more to do with personality difficulties. This is less easily resolved. If there is a running conflict between a small number of people, it is best to ask each of them how they perceive the trouble, and then perhaps try to bring them together for a discussion, if possible with someone who has training and experience as a counsellor.

It can, of course, be just as difficult if people get too friendly! I have never knowingly been at an event at which two participants married to other people shared a bed, but I have heard from other leaders of it happening. I am not sure how I would deal with it, but if it were causing scandal among the group, then I would probably at least ask them to desist or leave.

Do not let this section worry you! Real problems are very unusual when running a residential event. Most people who go to a retreat or Christian conference are cooperative and are there to pray and learn. If problems do occur, they are usually minor, and can be sorted out with common sense and good communications.

SOME IDEAS FOR RETREATS AND CONFERENCES

This book contains detailed plans for only a small number of retreats and conferences. The list of possible ways of using a time away is, however, endless, and only a small selection of them can be described. Among the following ideas, you may find something which sparks off some enthusiasm in you, or which you recognize as a need in your own church. If you want to try and work with one of these ideas, call together a group of people and work through the planning process suggested.

Weekends on spirituality and the arts are very popular. Preparation for this type of retreat involves providing the setting and the materials for people to reflect creatively about their environment, their faith and their feelings. Not much direct input is needed, but you should have at least one artist who understands how to relate art and faith on hand to help and advise. I took part in a weekend at which we had a painter, a woodcarver, a dancer and a musician, each working with a small group of people. Some participants found that these activities helped them to break through to parts of their own spirituality which they had never before experienced; others found it silly!

Bringing together different groups within the community to discuss matters of common interest can be a valuable way of involving the Church in the locality, and of showing that Christianity has much to offer to life in today's world. Invite those involved in medicine, or education, or industry, or local politics to a sharing of views. See it as a time for the Church to learn and listen, as well as an opportunity to provide some direct Christian input. Such conferences can prove extremely fruitful and can increase cooperation between groups in the area, and can also raise the profile of the Church significantly.

Take away a group of those preparing for marriage — a number of churches in the area could well combine to make this an annual event. Sessions might include biblical teaching on marriage; finance; sexuality; society's expectations of marriage, etc. The local branch of RELATE may well be interested in helping to arrange this type of event.

Local Church members involved in similar jobs sometimes welcome the opportunity to share reflections on a Christian perspective on their work. Christian teachers, industrial workers, shopkeepers, farmers, nurses, and many other occupational groupings often find it helps them to develop their vocation to job and faith if they are brought together to explore biblical and Church insights and challenges.

Many Churches have experienced the benefits of taking a group of leaders away for residential training. Youth leaders, those working with children, musicians, discussion group leaders and others can have their ministry strengthened and broadened by a mixture of practical and reflective sessions. A large Church probably has enough leaders to make this a worthwhile exercise on its own; smaller Churches could combine with others in the area. Try to find someone with experience of the type of work under consideration to lead this sort of event.

Contemporary ethical problems provide fruitful material for a time away. The programme might focus on a single group of questions — the Christian response to war, for example, would give rise to discussions about pacifism, nuclear deterrence, the arms trade, etc. — or a range of problems may be addressed. Arrange for someone to give some input on insights from the Bible and Christian tradition, and invite someone with specific knowledge of the problems under discussion — up–to–date knowledge of the facts is very important in ethical study.

Communication skills are best taught in a residential setting, since this gives more time for participants to learn about many of the practical applications involved. The written word; compiling short talks for local radio; producing a Church magazine; using the voice in Church — most congregations have people who do these things regularly, and would benefit from more training. A local drama teacher, radio presenter or newspaper editor would probably be delighted to offer help.

Preparing for Easter, or preparing for Christmas, can be an excellent retreat theme. Spend time studying the relevant Bible passages, and allow ample time for silent reflection on the festivals. In some traditions, time could be given to the appropriate liturgical preparations.

A training weekend for evangelism would be a valuable tool to offer the local Church or group of Churches. This may be for a specific purpose, for example a missionary week in the locality, or it may be an event for anyone wishing to improve their personal evangelism. A wealth of material is produced by Bible Society, Scripture Union and the Church Pastoral Aid Society, among others.

Many people in the Churches would value a time away exploring what ministry God is calling them to. Some exposition of the Bible passages dealing with the divine call — of the prophets, Paul, Jesus — and an explanation of the varieties of ordained and lay ministry available in the Church might be combined with individual advice and group exploration of participants' vocations.

A poetry retreat could be arranged to reflect on poetry from within the Bible, and poetry from other sources, both Christian and non–Christian. The list of possible authors for inclusion is very wide. Try, for example, concentrating on twentieth–century poets such as T.S. Eliot, R.S. Thomas, W.H. Auden. *The New Oxford Book of Christian Verse,* edited by Donald Davie (Oxford University Press, 1981), contains more than enough material. Have copies of the poems to be used available for participants to reflect on in silence, and encourage them to write some poems of their own. Many people find that writing their own Psalm can be a moving experience.

Reading retreats are common. A group of people can meet to read the same book, and discuss it in groups as they progress through it, or they can read whatever they wish in peace and relative silence.

Someone with a wide knowledge of music might arrange a musical retreat. A choice of music reflecting a range of moods can be combined with readings and short imaginative and explanatory introductions.

The writings of some of the great mystics provide ample material for a retreat on exploring a range of methods of prayer. Try, for example, Meister Eckhardt, Hildegarde of Bingen, St John of the Cross, St Teresa of Avila. Short passages can be printed for participants, and meditations arranged in the style of each mystic.

A conference/retreat on Christian healing is always popular. A combination of prayer, Bible study and worship can form the basis for this, but do ensure that someone with long experience of this kind of ministry is included in the leadership team. It is a good idea to have a sympathetic Christian doctor present.

Growing older is an interesting topic for a group of senior members within the Church to explore, and can lead them to a greater sense of their value to God and to the Church. Remembering God's guidance in the past; looking forward; the Bible and ageing; and an appropriate spirituality for old age all lead to fruitful study.

Some Churches have invited a number of recently bereaved people to a time away. Scriptural passages on death and resurrection could form the backbone of this event, while time can also be given to individual counselling and to group discussion about the joys of the past, and the problems of being alone.

A similar weekend could be offered for Christians recently separated and divorced.

Icons offer an interesting and stimulating focus for a retreat. Someone skilled in their interpretation can not only throw light on the potential for meditation which they contain, but can also lead to discussion on the theology which lies behind them. Some participants may welcome the opportunity to paint their own icons.

Some centres may provide an ideal base for a pilgrimage retreat with participants spending time in a number of local holy places. Walks and prayer at these places could be combined with some input on the history and significance of the sites.

The Celtic spiritual tradition, which emphasizes seeing God's presence in the ordinary things of life, can be the basis for a retreat. An excellent book which gives many ideas for this is *A World Made Whole* by Esther de Waal (Fount, 1991).

Keeping a spiritual journal has become a popular theme for a weekend workshop. An honest chronicling of God's actions in one's daily life can be a great source of strength to many people. I. Progoff's book *At a Journal Workshop* (1975) gives many useful ideas.

A retreat/conference for married couples who wish to explore the significance of the Christian faith for their relationship can be arranged. Time can be given to the long tradition of Christian marriage. Make sure that at least one of the leaders has training and experience in marriage counselling.

STARTERS

Almost all residential events will benefit from an "ice breaking" activity at the beginning. Even retreats in which the majority of the time is to be spent in silence will go better for starting with this kind of exercise because participants will be able to relax into the silence more effectively if they know one another.

Most books of interactive games includes some ice breakers. The examples which follow are simple and effective.

The Name Game

This is a good way of helping people to learn one another's names quickly. The name game lasts about 15 minutes with twenty people.

Sit the participants in a circle. The first person says his name — "I'm David." The second repeats the first name, and adds her own — "He's David; I'm Mary." The third repeats the first two, and adds his own — "He's David, she's Mary; I'm John." This continues around the circle, until the first person has a second go. When someone forgets a name, they must start again from the first person, after being told the name they have forgotten.

Introducing each other

This starter does not encourage participants to learn all the names as quickly as the one above, but it does help them to find out more about some people than just their name. It takes about 30 minutes.

Divide into pairs, and ask each member to talk about herself for 5 minutes. Then each pair joins with another pair, and people take it in turns to introduce their partner to the other pair, including as much detail as possible. It time allows, groups of eight can then be formed, with each person introducing one of the other pair to the new group.

Bingo

Give a bingo card to everyone — you can photocopy the one in this book, or invent your own to fit the group. Make sure there are enough pens or pencils available. This game takes about 20 minutes with twenty people.

Everyone mills around, asking others one question at a time from the card. If the person answers yes, put their name in the box. They may then ask a question in return. After one question each, move on to other people. The same name cannot appear more than three times on anyone's card. The first to complete their card calls "Bingo", and the game stops.

collects stamps	is an eldest child	follows cricket	plays piano
has three children	rides a horse	is a keen gardener	can't swim
like brown sauce	smokes a pipe	goes fishing	sings in a choir
watches "Neighbours" on T.V.	reads detective novels	reads "The Times"	can't touch toes
likes jazz music	is left–handed	has ridden in a Rolls Royce	speaks a foreign language

Historical characters

Prepare a card bearing the name of a famous historical character for each participant. The cards are pinned on their backs, without them being allowed to see the name. Participants then go around the room asking questions which will help them to discover who they are. The only answers allowed are "yes" or "no". Participants may only ask one question at a time — then they must move on to another person. Continue until everyone has discovered their identity. This usually takes about 20 minutes with twenty people.

Names might include: Shakespeare; Julius Caesar; Atilla the Hun; Napoleon; Queen Victoria; Churchill; Cleopatra; Margaret Thatcher; etc.

Detective drawings

Each person is given a pencil and a sheet of paper. In pairs, who should not know each other well, each has five minutes to draw six objects which they have used in the last month. They must remain silent, while their partner tries to deduce as much as possible about the person from the drawings. After 5 minutes change roles. At the end of the second 5 minutes participants should briefly introduce their partner to the whole group, based on what they have discovered through the drawings. This game takes about 30 minutes with twenty people.

What's my line?

Arrange the group so that everyone has a good view of each other. In turn, each person is asked to mime an interest or hobby, while others try to guess what is being mimed. This could be played two or three times, depending on the time available and the size of the group. It usually takes about 2 minutes per participant for each to have one turn.

GAMES FOR LEARNING AND FOR FUN

There is a large number of games available for using at residential events. Games should not be seen as an end in themselves, but as aids to learning and interaction. Careful choice of appropriate games, and meticulous preparation are important. If possible, you should have taken part in any game before attempting to lead it yourself — even a run–through with your planning group is better than nothing.

GAMES HAVE A NUMBER OF DIFFERENT USES:

- They can be a good way of relaxing people and helping them to mix at the beginning of an event.
- They often help participants to talk openly about deep feelings.
- They can be used to simulate events in real life.
- They can be fun — don't underestimate the importance of this element.

Don't be afraid to modify games to suit your own needs. Many games have been picked up, passed on and altered many times as leaders find new angles on the same game. Part of the interest generated by games is inventing your own and modifying others.

The following is a short selection of games which are suitable for use at residential events. They have been chosen to show the range available, and because I have used all of them and found them to work well. At the end of this section some useful books of games are mentioned. There are many books available — diocesan/area resource centres are often a good sources of game books.

What's it worth?

Purpose: To encourage members to consider their priorities in life, and to provide a discussion starter

Time: About 1 hour — 30 minutes for the activity and 30 minutes for discussion.

Method: Ask everyone to write down in CAPITAL LETTERS the six most important things in their lives. These can include people, possessions, ideas, faith, occupation, etc. They should be written in straight lines across the page with a gap of at least 1" between. Then ask participants to tear the sheet into strips, each strip containing one thing precious to them. The group should imagine that they are asked by God to give up one of these things for him. Ask each person, one by one, to put one of their strips into the middle of the group, leaving the five most precious things in their hand. Repeat this process until each person has only one strip, with their most precious thing written on it.

This can be varied according to how well known to each other members of the group are. The game can, for example, be played with members announcing what is written on each strip as they place it in the centre, or remaining silent.
Discussion should focus on people's feelings as they make decisions about what to give up. What are the criteria for their decisions?

Picking pictures

Purpose: To create group identity. To start discussion about how decisions are made.

Time: About 30 minutes for the exercises. It can be followed by discussion for up to another 30 minutes.

Preparation: Prepare a number of pictures or posters and distribute them around the room. There should be enough pictures for two per participant, with about a dozen extra. They can be from a variety of sources and sizes, but should depict a wide range of subjects and styles.

Method: Each person chooses two pictures or posters which they feel are saying something to them. When the choice has been made, each member finds a partner. Using whatever method they wish, each pair chooses two of their four pictures to keep, and two to discard. Each pair then finds another pair, and again the new groups each choose two pictures to keep and two to reject. Groups of eight are then formed, and the process repeated until the whole group joins together and decides on the two pictures it wishes to keep.

Discussion should focus on the methods of decision making rather than the merits of particular pictures.

All sorts

Purposes: To help members think about the workings of the group and their own place in it.

Time: About 20 minutes.

Preparation: On a large piece of card or paper draw circles — some by themselves, some in clusters, some in pairs, some overlapping. Have a few more circles than there are people in the group. Number each circle. The example shows how this might be drawn. Have pens and paper ready.

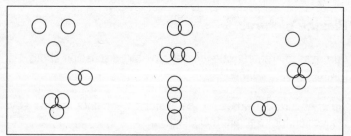

Method: Explain that the circles represent people.
- Ask each member to note down privately which circle they identify with themselves.
- Ask each member to note down which circles they identify with other group members.

- Ask anyone who wants to to add a circle in silence — it may represent themselves or someone else in the group.
- Ask each member to note down privately which circle they would like to be identified with.

Discussion can focus on perceptions of ourselves and others, and of the patterns which form within groups.

Sharing resources

Purposes: This exercise is useful on a Church conference because it provides a list of skills and interests of members.

Time: About 30 minutes.

Method: In small groups of up to eight people, each member in turn should describe the skills, knowledge and interests he or she has. These are listed on a large sheet of paper. Everything should be included, however trivial or esoteric it may seem. After an initial round of everyone, ask people to add things they have subsequently thought of. Encourage spontaneity and discourage modesty.

Retain the list for later use when particular skills are likely to be needed.

Trading game

Purpose: To help members appreciate the complexities of world trade. To begin discussion about the way groups interact.

Time: About 1 hour.

At least twenty people are needed to play this game, but preferably no more than forty.

Preparation: Divide the group into five equally sized small groups, each representing a nation. Ensure that the members of the groups do not bring any materials such as pencils or scissors into the room with them. Give the groups the following materials:

Group A:	10 sheets A4 card
	1 pair scissors
	10 money counters each worth £100
Group B:	10 sheets A4 card
	20 money counters each worth £100
	10 money counters each worth £50
Group C:	5 sheets A4 Card
	1 pair scissors
	1 compass
	1 ruler
Group D:	2 pencils
	2 pairs scissors
	2 compasses
	1 protractor
	1 sheet A4 card
	1 money counter worth £100
	1 ruler
Group E:	5 pencils
	1 pair scissors
	1 compass
	10 counters each worth £50
	1 ruler

The leader is also the Bank, or it can be operated by someone else.

Each nation must manufacture products according to international standards as set out on the sheet, of which each group has one copy. Manufactured goods may be deposited with the Bank at their face value, as may money. There is no fixed trading price for tools or resources.

The purpose of the game is for nations to trade and manufacture goods. The nation with the highest cash balance in the Bank at the end of the set time is the winner.

Body talk

Purpose: To help participants appreciate the importance of communication.

Time: About 45 minutes.

Numbers: Groups of about six to ten people.

Preparation: Prepare a set of 52 cards (more will be needed if there are more than eight players), about 4" x 3". Divide the pack into three piles. Draw one of the following symbols, representing hand, face and whole body, in the lower half of the cards in each pile. In the upper half write an emotion — anger, insecurity, love, hate, shame, jealousy, fear, joy, etc.

Deal six cards to each player after shuffling the pack, and place the remainder face down in a pile. The first person to get rid of his or her cards is the winner.

The first player chooses a card from her hand, and lays it face down in front of her. She uses the part of the body drawn on the card to express the emotion written on the card.

If other players think that they hold a card with the emotion being expressed written on it (but not necessarily the same part of the body), they should place it face down in front of them. All cards are turned face up at the same time.

If one or more of the others matches the emotion on the card of the player, she puts it and all the matching cards at the bottom of the pile. Any person who puts down a card which does not match the player's must return it to his hand, and draw an additional card from the deck. If no-one matches the player's card, she returns the card to her hand and draws a penalty card. In this case, others return their cards to their hand, but do not draw a penalty.

Tell us the story of. . .

Purpose: To begin members thinking about their own spiritual
journey, and the journeys of others.

Time: About 1 hour.

This game is best played in groups of four to six people.

A game board similar to that below should be made for each
group, or this can be photocopied. The squares can be adapted
to suit the needs of those playing. Each player has a button or
other counter, and each group needs a die. When a player lands
on a square with words, he should follow the instructions, and
tell the group the story of the event described.

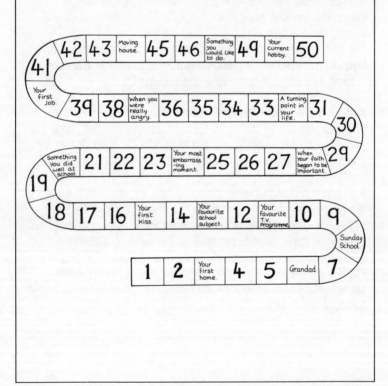

Physical opinions

Purpose: To enable group members to express their opinions
on a range of subjects quickly, and to stimulate discussion. This
activity also has the advantage that it ensures that people move
around, and thus can be useful in the middle of a session which
consists mostly of talk.

Time: 5 — 10 minutes.

Designate opposite ends of the room as extreme opinions, with
shades of opinion being placed at intermediate points.
Members should go to a place in the room which reflects their
view. For example, if abortion is under discussion, one end of
the room would be that abortion is never permissible, the other
end that abortion should be freely available on demand.
Someone who felt that abortion should be available in the case
of rape or danger to the mother's health would be closer to, but
not at, the "never" end. Opinions about a number of different
issues can be expressed in a short time.

People can be asked to explain precisely what their position
means, and to justify why they are there.

Obituary

Purpose: To enable reflection about oneself. This is a useful
exercise for a reflective and prayerful weekend, and is probably
best used in the middle of the residential period rather than at
the beginning or end.

Time: About 30 minutes for writing, followed by time for
sharing.

Each person is to write their own obituary on no more than two
sides of A4. It is not to be the obituary you fear might be written
about you, but the obituary you would most like. You are to let
your fancy run free — write about the person you would like to
be rather than the person you really are.

Allow time for discussion and reflection either in pairs or in
groups of three or four.

BOOKS

There is a large number of books about games available. The following are particularly useful:

Games for Social and Life Skills by Tim Bond, (Hutchinson, 1986).

Simulation Games (3 Volumes) by Pat Baker and Mary–Ruth Marshall, (Joint Board of Christian Education, Melbourne, 1986).

ENDINGS

The final session of a residential time is important. Not only should there be a way of finishing the group's time together, but it also provides opportunities for members to begin to think of how they will take what they have learned or prayed into their everyday lives. Further, it can be a time of learning for the leaders as they listen to the reactions of those who have taken part.

An ending can be simple — two people telling each other how they have found the experience — or it can be a carefully structured and complex game. In most cases, the simple ending is better.

Most of the endings which follow fulfil the two aims of reflecting on the time together, and looking forward to daily life.

Taking a message home

The leader invites participants to write two messages they want to pass on when they return home as a result of the time away. One message is to their husband/wife/friend, and the other is to their vicar/priest/minister. After about five minutes to write the messages, each member of the group reads out their own messages.

This ending takes about 10 minutes for the explanation and writing, plus a maximum of 2 minutes for each participant to read out what they have written. You may wish to allow time for general discussion after all the messages have been read out.

Positive feelings

We are usually quick to criticize others, but find praising them difficult and embarrassing. This exercise encourages members to look for the good in others, and can ensure that the time together finishes on a high note.

Each person has a large sheet of paper, and writes their name at the top. The paper is passed around the circle, and each member must write a positive comment about the person whose name is at the top. At the end, each person reads the comments addressed to him or her in silence.

> This ending takes about 2 or 3 minutes for each participant.
>
> A variant of this ending is to pin a piece of paper on each person's back. The participants must write their positive comments on the backs of each of their fellow members.

The following three endings are taken from Games for Social and Life Skills by Tim Bond (Hutchinson, 1986).

While we have been together

Materials: Copies of prepared cards (see examples below).

Time: About 3–4 minutes per person.

Procedure:
1. Arrange the group in a circle. Place the cards in a pile face down in the centre.
2. Each person takes a card in turn and answers the question as honestly as they can. The question applies only to the time the group have been together for the course.
3. After each person has spoken as prompted by their card, the others can ask questions to check points that are not clear.
4. Pass to the next person until everyone has had a turn.

Examples for cards:
While we have been together:
- the thing that made me most angry was . . .
- the funniest thing was . . .
- the thing I regret most . . .
- I was upset when . . .
- the most interesting thing was . . .
- the person who was kindest to me . . .
- the thing which made me most nervous was . . .
- the most valuable experience was . . .
- my best memory is . . .
- the person I wish I had got to know better . . .
- the thing I would most like to repeat . . .
- the thing which interested me least . . .
- the thing which made me angry with myself was . . .
- the thing I most disliked was . . .
- the thing which frustrated me was . . .
- the thing I would like to do more of . . .
- the thing I would like to do less of . . .
- the thing that made me happy was . . .
- the person who has been a good friend . . .

Achievements

Materials: Blackboard or flipchart to display questions.

Time: 30–40 minutes.

Procedure:
1. Divide into groups of three to five people.
2. Ask them to take turns in discussing these questions:
   • What did I hope to achieve when I began this course?
   • What do I feel I have achieved in the course?
   • What will I try to do differently because of the course?
   • What do I plan to do next to build on the course or satisfy unmet needs?

Participants should to help each other with the last two questions. The aim is that each person can see the practical implications of the course for themselves and they plan what they will do next to follow it up. This may include promising to tell a friend in a week's or a month's time how they feel the course has affected them, or how they have achieved a personal goal.

3. The leader can circulate to help the discussions and if necessary ask the groups to come back into the large group and summarize their discussions and conclusions.

Reflections

Time: About 2–3 minutes per person.

Procedure:
1. Ask the group to sit in a circle and explain:
This is your opportunity to say what your strongest impression of the time we have spent together is. I want each of you in turn to imagine you are driving away in a car, and you look back in the mirror and see this course. What is the strongest image you see reflected in the mirror? It can be a feeling or an event. After you have spoken, the others can ask questions about what you have said.
2. Work round the group in turn, or let people respond when they are ready until everyone has had a turn.

Goal–setting

Time: This will vary according to the number of goals to be set. Allow about 10 minutes for one goal per person; about 20 minutes for three. If a large group is working on goals, then a full session of 1½ hours may be needed.

This method of ending is an attempt to set firm goals for the future. It is appropriate both for individual spiritual goals, and for group goals such as planning for a Church.

The exercise can be simple or complex, depending on the number of goals to be set, and on the time scale to be looked at.

At its simplest, ask participants to set one goal, and state how they will achieve the goal, and when they aim to achieve it by. If more than one goal is to be set, then a chart can be offered as a way of formulating the ideas:

What I will do?	How I will do it?	When I will do it by?

If this exercise is to be used, for example, by a group planning for the next five years for a Church, different areas of work might each have their own chart — worship, finance, property, mission, education, etc.

What I have been told

Time: About 2–3 minutes per person. If done in pairs, it should take no more than 6 minutes.

This ending should only be used in a group where people know each other well and have built up a high degree of trust and openness. If you are not certain that this degree of trust exists, the ending might work well in pairs or groups of three or four. It is an ending which is especially appropriate to a retreat or time of spiritual reflection.

Ask the participants to share with the group something which the Lord has told them during the times of prayer. Each person's contribution should not be commented on, simply received in silence with a small gap between each person for reflection.

METHODS OF REFLECTION

USING SILENCE WHILE AWAY

For many people a long period of silence is an unknown experience, and they can be anxious at the very idea of it. It used to be the practice on all retreats to have very long, very strict silences. You might arrive on Friday evening, and be allowed to talk quietly to fellow retreatants over dinner, but you would then be expected to remain silent until lunch on Sunday. Not surprisingly, this prevented many people from learning the value of silence. For those new to silence, it should be introduced gently. Suggest short periods of silence — begin with perhaps 10 minutes, and build up to 1 hour during the weekend. Give participants something specific to do in the silence; describe an exercise or a topic for meditation, and encourage people to discuss the experience with one or two others afterwards.

Practical difficulties may be the greatest stumbling block to the creative use of silence, with mealtimes presenting the most problems. How can I get my hands on the salt, which is firmly set at the other of the table? Should I gesticulate wildly, or reach rudely across while others are eating? Learning to wait patiently may be a valuable lesson, and if we are unable to express our own needs, we may become more aware of the needs of others. Observing our neighbours' needs, and waiting on them, we get to know them in a different way from talking to them. Do not worry when people are attacked by uncontrollable laughter — this frequently happens in groups which are new to silence. An antidote to this is "partial silence", in which participants are allowed to talk when necessary, but are encouraged to maintain silence otherwise.

Recent years have seen a great explosion in the number of books published which concentrate on Christian methods of meditation and reflection. Much of the impetus behind this growth has been the increase of interest shown in *The Spiritual Exercises of St Ignatius,* and some of the methods described here are firmly located in that tradition. It is remarkable, however, that the value of such approaches is by no means confined to the more catholic branches of the Church. All sections of the Church have realized that most of these styles of prayer and meditation are deeply scriptural and provide a way of coming to grips with the faith which is acceptable to catholics and evangelicals alike.

Most of the approaches described below can be used in almost any retreat or conference, either as part of the time set aside for worship, or as an introduction to a meditative session.

The advantage of teaching people to use these approaches in a residential setting is that they are free from the distractions of ordinary life, and they have the time to explore the methods fully.

Whichever styles of meditation are used, the same introductory points apply. It is worth giving time to explaining these.

1. The practicalities of place and posture are very important. Find a place to pray which fits your needs of stillness and quiet, and in which you are not likely to be distracted. The best posture is that which enables you to be attentive and relaxed at the same time. This varies from person to person, but you should above all aim at a posture which allows you to be still. Some sit cross-legged; some lie down — this is good if you can do it without falling asleep; some sit on their heels. Perhaps it is easiest to sit on an upright chair with a straight back and both feet flat on the ground.

2. Remember that all methods of prayer are a means to an end. No one method works miracles, and they all need practice before you feel at home in them — don't discard a method after one try. Be patient and persevere for a while.

3. Give time to preliminaries before prayer. Choose where to pray. Settle into a posture; still your body and mind. Recognize the presence of God. Offer the time to him, and ask for his light and for openness. It has been said that if you have 10 minutes for prayer, you spend 9 minutes getting ready and 1 minute actually praying.

Exercises for stillness

These three approaches can be just relaxing exercises; attentive preparations for other kinds of prayer; or, in themselves, a still, attentive, wordless prayer of presence. Each of the following three exercises should take between 10 and 20 minutes.

Awareness of the body

Sitting upright in a chair, with your feet flat on the ground, and with a straight back, relax each part of the body in turn. Start from the crown of the head, and pass through each part to the feet. Be aware of the touch of clothes, the feel of the chair, etc. Do this two or three times, recognizing God's presence in your feelings, in your body, and in you as a person.

Awareness of sounds

Sitting in a relaxed posture, identify each sound you can hear. Do not rush, as many sounds only become apparent with attentive listening. Concentrate the attention wholly on each sound, and then move on. Sudden sounds or distractions should be acknowledged, but not fought against. Recognize God's presence in the sounds, and in what they symbolize — people, nature, etc. This exercise might lead naturally to thanks or praise, and also to a realization of how dulled our senses have become, and how little we listen to God. This exercise works best if traffic noise is avoided!

Breathing

Again sitting in a relaxed posture, listen to your own breathing. Do not alter the pace or the depth (this is difficult to start with), but just be aware and concentrate all your attention on this one action. If you are distracted, do not fight. Acknowledge the distraction and pass back to focussing on your breathing. This can develop in two ways:
God is my breathing . . . God is as the air I breath . . . all around, and within me . . . source of all life . . . breathe out desire and selfishness . . . In . . . out; receive . . . offer.

Another way is to link each breath with a word or phrase of a prayer. The Lord's prayer can be said or thought word by word or phrase by phrase as you breathe in and out. The Orthodox "Jesus Prayer" consists of repeating the phrase "Lord Jesus, have mercy on me a sinner" with each breath. Many biblical phrases and prayers can be used in this way — it is especially good with verses from the Psalms.

Praying the scriptures

The following methods of prayer will all be more effective if you use one of the exercises for stillness described above first. Prepare the chosen passage by reading it and becoming familiar with it. During prayer, you may wish to note any interesting intellectual questions, but shelve them, and do not try to answer them during prayer.

A *"savouring prayer"*. Read a passage of scripture slowly until a word or phrase particularly strikes you. Savour the word or phrase by vocally or mentally repeating it until it fills your consciousness, and either you begin to speak spontaneously to the Lord in whose presence you are, or you simply rest before him in silence. When you have found all you can, or you are distracted, pass back to the slow reading until another word or phrase strikes you. You do not have to finish your chosen passage. Be content even if you do not need to go beyond the first word.

Gospel contemplation. This approach uses the imagination to bring gospel scenes into our present. It has a long history and was used by the early Cistercians and Franciscans before being made the centre of Ignatius Loyola's Exercises. An example using a specific passage is given in the weekend of Spiritual Reflection (see chapter 13).

1. Take a gospel scene and read it carefully a few times to familiarize yourself with it. You may prefer to use the text when praying, but it is probably better to work from memory — find whichever way is best for you.

2. Imagine yourself in the scene. Take time, and use your senses. If the story is set near the Sea of Galillee then see it, smell it, listen to the water. Get into a boat and feel it rocking; taste the salt spray on your lips. When the scene is present to you, then go on.
3. Let the story play itself through with you in it. You may instinctively become a central character, for example, Peter in the boat, or someone asking for healing. Or you may be a bystander, a person in a crowd. Don't worry if you want to change roles — often the unplanned is an indication that you are really involved. Hear the words spoken; see people's actions and reactions. Allow your reactions to happen. If you have any questions, address them to Jesus.
4. You may find that you converse with Jesus or with others in the story quite naturally. In any case, when the scene is over, take time to address Jesus face to face. If there is something you don't understand question him. End by asking yourself what you must do as a result of this encounter.

The following passages of Scripture are listed in *God of Surprises* by Gerard W. Hughes, (Darton, Longman and Todd, 1985) pages 125–126. They lend themselves especially well to this type of prayer, as do many other narrative sections:

The infancy and hidden life
Luke 1.26–38 The message to Mary is that she is to bear a child. Christ is still coming to birth in you and me.
Luke 1.46–55 Mary's delight in her poverty: 'My heart praises the Lord; my soul is glad because of God my saviour.'
Luke 2.1–20 The birth of Christ.
Luke 2.22–35 Jesus is presented in the Temple, and Simeon takes the child in his arms and prophesies. The prophecy is still being fulfilled in us.
Luke 2.41–52 Jesus is found in the Temple. 'I must be about the affairs of my Father' — the theme of his life and ours, which causes a row even in the most perfect of families!

The public life
Matthew 3.13–17 Jesus leaves home for the Jordan. Walk with him. Jesus is baptized. We are plunged into that same life. Hear the Father saying to you. 'This is my own dear son.'

Matthew 4.1–11 Jesus is tempted in the desert. His temptations are ours too.

John 2.1–12 The first miracle at Cana.

Luke 4.16–30 Jesus at first welcomed, then rejected at Nazareth.

John 1.35–51 The call of the first disciples. How do you react when this call is addressed to you?

Luke 5.1–11 The call of Peter.

Luke 6.17–49 Jesus preaching

Luke 10.38–42 Jesus with friends — Martha and Mary.

John 4.1–42 Jesus and the outsider — with the woman at the well.

Matthew 14.13–21 Jesus feeds the five thousand.

Matthew 14.22–33 Jesus walks on the water, which symbolizes all the powers of chaos and destruction. Jesus calls, 'Courage, it is I. Don't be afraid.' He is still calling to us, 'Come'.

THE FOUR ANCHOR POINTS OF PRAYER

Too often we rush into prayer, without giving any thought to how we will approach and use the time. A residential event gives us time to consider our approach more carefully than is possible in the business of daily life. Here is a suggested way of preparing for and reflecting on prayer in four easily remembered stages.

Preparation

Before beginning to pray, ask yourself the following questions:
1. How am I feeling? What sort of mood am I in? How is this likely to affect my prayer?
2. What do I want to ask the Lord for? Peace? Generosity? Openness? Forgiveness?
3. What scripture text/hymn/poem shall I use?

Slow entry into prayer

1. Choose your place of prayer and go to it.

2. Make yourself comfortable, and become still, perhaps by using one of the stillness exercises.
3. If you find it helpful, make a very slow sign of the cross (either external or mental), and slowly ask the Holy Spirit to help you pray.

PRAYER

Slow exit from prayer

1. Quietly bring your prayer together, being careful not to rush the ending.
2. Slowly say the Lord's Prayer, or read a short passage of Scripture.
3. Slowly leave the place where you have been praying thanking God for the time he has been with you.

Review or reflection after prayer

In a different place from where you have been praying, slowly recall the prayer period, rather like a video replay of the highlights of your prayer.

- Was it good to be at prayer, or not?
- Why?
- What did you do at the beginning of prayer?
- Did you learn something during prayer?
- Did the Lord ask something of you?
- Did you find any unwillingness in yourself to face what the Lord seemed to want of you?
- How did you close your period of prayer?

REVIEWING THE DAY

We have to be in touch with our feelings to sort them out and avoid being blown about by them. We experience God's action in our feelings, moods and desires just as much as in external events and ideas. At the level of our deeper and more lasting feelings we discover ourselves and our real relationship with god. It is, therefore, important that we should establish a routine of looking back over each day to see how our relationship with God had developed.

Begin by relaxing into God's presence.

Look over all the events and experiences of the day, especially noting particularly moods, feelings and desires. Did I experience joy, pain, love, anger, frustration, peace, loneliness, freedom . . . ?
Focus particularly on the more significant or dominant moods and experiences.

If I am unsettled, unhappy or feeling isolated can I identify the cause? If I am deep down contented and happy do I recognize the reasons? The Lord wishes me to be contented, and a settled feeling might be one sign that I am following God's will for me.

Ask yourself the following questions:
Where did I meet God's love today; in a friend, an event, and experience or beauty or in prayer?
Where have I been a sign of God's love to the people in my life today?
Where did I go out to the lonely, the sorrowful, the discouraged, the needy etc.?
Was I aware of God working in my own locality, my country, other nations of the world, or the Church?

Then look with gratitude on the day that has passed.

Thanksgiving will help us to discover God's daily gifts — gifts of our own qualities and those of others, of joys, and even the harsh and painful aspects of life which can also lead us to the Father.

My response in gratitude and sorrow

I thank the Lord for all that has been offered to me today, and for the occasions when I responded in love. I ask for a true awareness of my sinfulness, a sorrow for the ways in which I have failed to respond to love at work in me. I ask for a deep sense of being accepted and loved by the Lord, regardless of my response to his Love.

For the future, I ask for a greater sensitivity to the presence of God around me, and a development of my own desire and ability to respond to God.

My spiritual journey

This is a useful reflective exercise which can be done during a residential event by individuals for their own use, or as a basis for sharing and discussion.

Materials: Sheets of paper — probably A3 is about the right size — crayons, felt–tipped pens or pastels.

Method: Ask group members to take about 15 minutes to jot down on paper the spiritual ups and downs in their lives. Significant moments of growth and setback, new insights and changes of direction, people who were important influences — all these can be noted.

Then take about another 15 minutes to draw this journey as a road map. It could show the mountain tops, the dark valleys, the wrong turnings, the meanderings, etc. At significant points draw a symbol, or a person, or a signpost, to tell the story of the journey.

The results can be kept private, for reflection and prayer, or they can be shared with partners or in small groups.

What's blocking me?

Give each person a sheet of A3 paper or card and some coloured pastels or crayons — preferably one set per person. Ask participants to divide the sheet of paper into four sections, and head each section as follows:

My life as it is now

My life as I would like it to be

What's blocking me?

What do I need to overcome the block?

In each box, participants are asked to draw a picture or a symbol appropriate to the heading. Allow about 30 minutes for the drawing.

This exercise can be used as a starter for discussion in pairs, in small groups of no more than five, or it can be a valuable tool to use on its own for individuals.

Stories and humour

Do not underestimate the importance of using humour, even in "serious" periods of silence, meditation and worship. Anthony de Mello, for example, has written and collected a large number of stories which take us to the heart of Christian experience. These stories have the power to make people reassess their assumptions — a necessary part of all retreat work. Such stories are very effective as a means of lightening a talk, and they are so easy to remember that they will stick in people's minds for weeks. One word of caution — I used "the elephant and the rat" during an evening act of worship, and almost had to abandon the service because people could not stop laughing! Two short examples, taken from The Song of the Bird (Doubleday, 1984), give the flavour of de Mello's books.

The Elephant and the Rat

An elephant was enjoying a leisurely dip in a jungle pool when a rat came up to the pool and insisted that the elephant get out.

'I won't,' said the elephant.

'I insist that you get out this minute,' said the rat.

'Why?'

'I shall tell you that only after you are out of the pool.'

'Then I won't get out.'

But he finally lumbered out of the pool, stood in front of the rat, and said, 'Now then, why did you want me to get out of the pool?'

'To check if you were wearing my swimming trunks,' said the rat.

An elephant will sooner fit into the trunks of a rat than God will fit into our notions of him.

The Talkative Lover

A lover pressed his suit successfully for many months, suffering the atrocious pains of rejection. Finally his sweetheart yielded. 'Come to such and such a place at such and such an hour,' she said to him.

At that time and place the lover finally found himself seated beside his beloved. He then reached into his pocket and pulled out a sheaf of love letters that he had written to her over the past months. They were passionate letters, expressing the pain he felt and his burning desire to experience the delights of love and union. He began to read them to his beloved. The hours passed by, but still he read on and on.

Finally the woman said, 'What kind of a fool are you? These letters are all about me and your longing for me. Well, here I am sitting with you at last and you are lost in your stupid letters.

'Here I am with you,' says God, 'and you keep reflecting about me in your head, talking about me with your tongue, and searching for me in your books. When will you shut up and see?'

BOOKS

There are many books on the market which contain material suitable for using at residential retreats. The following list is a selection which I have found especially useful.

Deeper into God by Brother Ramon SSF, (Marshall, Morgan and Scott, 1987). Brother Ramon is a widely acknowledged expert on leading retreats. This book gives valuable insights into withdrawing and the use of silence, but does not address the practicalities.

The Study of Spirituality by Cheslyn Jones, Geoffrey Wainwright and Edward Yarnold (eds.), (1986). An excellent and comprehensive introduction to Christian spirituality throughout the ages. If you are searching for leads on new ideas from the past, this is ideal.

Awareness by Anthony de Mello, (HarperCollins, 1990). Anthony de Mello, a Jesuit who combined eastern and western traditions, is one of the "guru" figures of contemporary spirituality. His other books, including *Sadhana, One Minute Wisdom,* and *The Song of the Bird,* are all goldmines for short, thought–provoking stories.

Meditating as a Christian by Peter Toon, (Collins 1991). A good introduction to a range of methods for meditation on Scripture from a noted evangelical Anglican writer.

God of Surprises by Gerard W. Hughes, (Darton, Longman and Todd, 1985). Already a great classic of the spiritual journey.

This book not only contains excellent guidance for the individual, but is also a fund of ideas and suggestions and ideas for retreats.

Three very useful books are *Listening to God, Open to God,* and *The Smile of Love* by Joyce Huggett (Hodder and Stoughton, 1988 — 1990). They introduce a variety of methods of reflection, and produce excellent biblically based meditations. The first book is accompanied by a tape.

A Transforming Friendship by James Houston, (Lion, 1991) is aimed at the individual's exploration of prayer, but many of the ideas are valuable for use in the context of a group retreat. Some of the chapters would make a good basis for introductory talks on various aspects of spirituality.

Exercises for Stillness, Praying the Scriptures, The Four Anchor Points of Prayer, and *Reviewing the Day* are based on talks and duplicated notes by Fr Damian Jackson SJ given to a retreat for the Gloucester and Hereford School for Ministry.

What's Blocking Me? is based on a session at a retreat led by the Revd. Robert Horsfield for the Gloucester and Hereford School of Ministry.

TIMES AWAY FOR ALL AGES

An increasing number of churches are organizing residential events for members across the age range. These have many advantages; not least that families are enabled to explore their faith together in a relaxed setting.

There are many good books available which give ideas for worship and activities for all–age groups, (see chapter 12 for more details), so I will not attempt to give many ideas here.

Decisions to be made about an all–age weekend are:
• Will all the activities and learning be shared, or should the group be split up for much of the time?
• Is a common theme to be followed by all the ages?
• Will a crèche be needed for very small children?

Many of the practical arrangements are the same as those outlined in the opening chapters, but it is important to ensure that there are enough leaders — activities will need more leaders than you think. Do not try to cover too much when working with an all–age group; remember that much of the purpose is to have fun together rather than to plough through a set amount of work. Be relaxed — encourage parents to attend to the needs and interests of their children.

Most of the themes suggested in Chapter Six can be used with all–age groups, but themes based on Bible stories and those centred on Christian festivals work particularly well.

Two activities — mask making and banner making — are always popular in all–age residentials, and they can both be adapted to many themes.

Using masks in drama

This description is taken from *Show Me* by Judy Gattis Smith, and although she applies it primarily to work with children, it is equally good with a mixed group.

Masks have been used in drama for thousands of years. Greek actors performed entirely behind masks. Actors travelling round medieval Europe, conveyed stock characters — the grumbler, the miser, the teacher — by the use of masks which their international audiences would instantly recognize. The modern mime uses masks to highlight the use of the body.

In the classroom masks have other advantages. Making the masks helps children explore the story. The masks' exaggerated expressions can help children express the way a character feels. Under cover of a mask people find it easier to participate in drama.

Just as with puppets, there are many ways to create masks. Simple masks can be made from paper plates, pillow cases or paper bags. More elaborate masks can be constructed from papier–mâché or expanded polystyrene. For older children the make–up of circus clowns — the whiteface and the tramp — can be used as a simple mask.

Making a mask.

For a simple mask you will need a large *paper* bag for each person — it should be as thick and firm as possible — some scissors and thick felt–tipped pens or crayons.

The first step is to cut the mask to size. Cut off a strip all the way around the bottom of the bag so that it will rest well down on the shoulders without flopping or twisting. Slip the bag over the head, and carefully mark where the eyes and nose are. Take off the bag and cut out holes at the spots you have marked. When the holes are cut in the right places the masks can be decorated. If participants wish, they can glue things to the masks but the emotions will probably be better conveyed if drawn on with a pen or crayon.

Example: Happy and sad (John 11.28–44)

Aims: To express the feelings of some people Jesus helped. To decorate a mask.

How to do it: Tell a story from the Gospels which contains strong feelings — e.g. the story of Lazarus (John 11.28–44).

Everyone chooses a character, and must decorate two masks for that character. They must decorate one with a happy face and one with a sad face.

Participants then take it in turns to wear each mask and say why they feel that way. For example, Martha — sad because of the death of Lazarus; happy because Lazarus is alive.

Variations Other suitable stories are: Jesus heals ten men (Luke 17.11–19); the lost sheep (Luke 15.1–7); the lost coin (Luke 15.8–10).

If your group know the Bible well, you you can ask them to pick a character from any Bible story they know and like and make two masks — happy and sad — for that character in the same way.

This method is endlessly versatile and useful whenever you wish to achieve some basic identification with the feelings expressed in a story. Happy and sad could be replaced by frightened and brave or nasty and nice!

Banner–making

Making banners is a popular activity in which all ages can join on equal terms. Many themes can be utilized. The following description, taken from *All Age Worship* by Maggie Durran suggests making a number of banners about the life of a particular church, and arranging them in the form of a train. If this is done at a residential event, it makes an interesting and informative display to mount in the church when the group returns home. This activity works best in groups of about six people.

Materials: Prepared banner backgrounds (see below for instructions on how to make these), fabric scraps which may be brought by workshop participants, scissors, water based PVA glue.

Note: The glue can easily seep through the hessian in the banner backgrounds, so put newspaper under each group banner before glueing.

Before the workshop, prepare the banner backgrounds. These are large rectangles of furnishing hessian. From a local upholstery shop, purchase a length of hessian: this should be 72" wide and of the lightest weight, and the cheapest for its area; this will be cut into pieces 36" x 27" — so on an estimate of the numbers of people you will have at your workshop calculate the amount you should buy. Cut the hessian into pieces of the stated size. Cut out circles of 5" diameter (13cm) from felt or other non–fraying fabric, for wheels. Cut two of these wheels for each banner. Cut strips, one for each group's banner background, 1" x 26" (2.5cm x 66cm). Glue two wheels and one strip (base of carriage) to each background, across the 27" side, which becomes the bottom of the picture. Use water–based PVA glue or fabric glue.

Each group is going to make a piece of a large banner. When all the pieces are put together the workshop participants will have a picture that illustrates the life of the church. It is important that each member of the group listens to all the other members of that group. No–one can know someone else's thoughts and opinions without first listening.

Each group should talk together about what the church is for. What has God called this church to be? What is this church especially good at doing? What is its mission? What does each group member think the church should be doing more of? One person in your group may take notes of everyone's ideas and as a group allow time for everyone's ideas and opinions. Don't criticize or ignore the contributions of other group members. Think of a way to represent your group's ideas on the banner. Do not use words, make your banner a picture. On the group's banner background you will find there are already the wheels and chassis for a train carriage. One group banner will represent the engine. When all the groups have finished the larger banner will show the church as a train that is travelling along; its pictures illustrating the work and worship of the church.

As each group finishes its banner hang them consecutively behind the engine, along one wall of the room which you are using.

You should allow at least 1½ hours for this activity.

BOOKS

All Age Worship by Maggie Durran, (Angel Press, 1987). This excellent book gives guidance on principles and practicalities of worship, and contains many ideas which can be used in activities for all ages.

Show me by Judy Gattis Smith, (Bible Society, 1985). A collection of drama techniques and examples which are easy to use and effective.

Discovering Together by Gregory McCormick, (St Paul Publications, 1989). Drama, activities, outlines for talks and other helpful suggestions.

WORSHIP ON RETREATS AND CONFERENCES

Periods of worship during retreats and conferences present great opportunities, and need to be carefully planned and thought through. They are not just slotted into the days, but must be an integral part of the whole residential experience. It is essential that those who are responsible for planning the worship understand the design and purpose of the event, and that they are given clear direction by the leadership team about what is needed. The flow of the programme may suggest a quiet, devotional act of worship at one point, or a more charismatic and exciting service may be appropriate, but it is important to ensure that the right sort of worship is prepared for each of the times allocated.

Participants in a residential event are usually more open to new ideas and experimentation, so take full advantage of this. You may like to encourage people to bring their musical instruments with them, or to come with ideas and resources which can be woven into the corporate worship. You should certainly take the opportunity to involve people in conducting worship who may be reluctant to do so in a large congregation at home. But be careful not to pressurize them too much — worrying about reading in the act of worship at the end of the retreat may destroy any sense of relaxation and tranquillity for some people.

Do take care over the setting for worship. If the Centre has a chapel, plan carefully how you would like the furniture arranged to fit the act of worship. Take care with the lighting — do you need subdued lighting to create a mood of quiet, or bright lighting for joy and excitement? It may be possible to worship outside — an open air eucharist can be a new and moving experience for many people. It can be helpful to have some focal point for members to concentrate on. Perhaps some candles, an icon, an arrangement of flowers, or items collected by members of the group while on walks can be put in the centre, or at a point all can easily see.

The leaders should take some resources for worship to the conference. These should not be difficult to put together — a variety of hymn and song books; perhaps some pieces of traditional choral music; some collections of prayers and meditations; some of the excellent "office books" now published; Bibles in different translations; some tapes or records which might include both classical and modern music. A list of useful material is suggested at the end of this chapter, and some suggestions for forms of worship which work particularly well in a residential setting have been included. The availability of a photocopier in the Centre should make the use of a variety of material easy (copyright permitting). If considerable use is being made of material, particularly music, which is new to most members, plan some time for rehearsal into the programme.

In almost all events, members should be deeply involved in the preparation and leadership of worship. There are a variety of ways of making sure this can happen:

- Some weeks before going away, call together a small group of those who will be there to plan the worship. Do not rely entirely on those who are known to have a particular interest in leading worship — this is a chance to try some fresh ideas and new people.
- On a longer event, you could allocate a small group of people to plan and lead worship for each day. Let them know well in advance how much time they will have, and what the theme of the day will be.
- Set up a music group. Any collection of people will contain a handful of competent musicians. Make sure they bring instruments and music with them, and allocate a place and a time for them to meet. Again, it is important that they are carefully briefed on what might be appropriate.
- If there are ongoing discussion groups, they might each be responsible for one or more acts of worship. This is a good way of linking the themes in discussion with the services.

Worship can be a sensitive topic. On one occasion it had been decided by the planning group that all the conference worship should use non–sexist language. Male biblical images for God would be used, but all references to "man", when it meant "humanity" would be deleted, and as far as possible language would be inclusive. This provoked a minor skirmish during a plenary session when a handful of traditionalists complained that the organizers had no right to "monkey about with the worship". A potentially explosive incident took place, however, in one of the groups. One act of worship each day was planned to take place in discussion groups. The group leader had taken a service from the Anglican Alternative Service Book, and had changed some of the language. One member objected, and others supported him. They demanded that the service be used in its usual form. Members of the group soon took sides. One party would be offended by the use of sexist language; the other side would be equally offended by changes in the traditional worship. The leader decided that if the group could not agree on its form of worship, it should remain silent for the 30 minutes allotted to the service. This seemed a sensible compromise, but one of the group left the conference immediately.

Recorded Music in Worship

Recorded music is a fruitful source of material for mood–setting and for reflection, but it does need to be chosen with care, and if you are playing it as part of a meditation or in an act of worship, make sure that the equipment is powerful enough for the room — nothing is worse than a small tape recorder at full volume. Leaders will all have their favourite pieces of music. Here I mention only a few pieces which I have used.

• Vaughan Williams' *The Lark Ascending* is an excellent piece to play while people are assembling. It helps collect the thoughts, and really does encourage the mind and soul to ascend.

• Parts of Vivaldi's *The Four Seasons* are also good to play while members assemble.

• Beethoven's *Symphony No 6* is especially good when thinking about God's creation.

• Mozart's *Symphony No 41* communicates a powerful sense of completion and fulfilment.

• Bruch's *Violin Concerto* — the struggle between violin and orchestra which is eventually resolved.

• Bach's *Double Violin Concerto in D Minor* — As Paul Iles writes in his book, *The Pleasure of God's Company* (Kevin Mayhew, 1990), this piece "provides a marvellous insight into the way two people can relate together in complete mutuality with intimacy, trust and joy. The movements also reflect many changing moods within such a relationship."

Do not neglect the possibility of using modern music. Benjamin Britten's *War Requiem* contains some almost unbearably moving penitential sections; the "Hosanna" in Andrew Lloyd Webber's *Requiem* is a joyous celebration in Caribbean rhythms, and parts of his *Jesus Christ, Superstar* are very thought–provoking. Other contemporary gospel musicals are also good sources.

You need not confine your choice to modern religious music — pop songs can also be used. I have, for example, used the song *Perhaps Love,* sung by Placido Domingo and John Denver — play it through, and then read out the words slowly, interspersed with biblical verses about love, read by another voice.

Perhaps Love

(Words and music by John Denver. © 1980 Cherry Lane Music Publishing Co. Inc.)

Perhaps love is like a resting place
A shelter from the storm
It exists to give you comfort
It is there to keep you warm
And in those times of trouble
When you are most alone
The memory of love will bring you home

"God is love, and whoever lives in love lives in union with God and God lives in union with him." 1 John 4.16

"God loved the world so much that he gave his only Son, so that everyone who believes in him may not die but have eternal life." John 3.16

Perhaps love is like a window
Perhaps an open door
It invites you to come closer
It wants to show you more
And even if you lose yourself and
don't know what to do
The memory of love will see you through

"As I have loved you, so you must love one another." John 13.34

Oh love to some is like a cloud
To some as strong as steel
For some a way of living
For some a way to feel
And some say love is holding on
And some say letting go
And some say love is ev'rything
Some say they don't know

"Who, then, can separate us from the love of Christ?" Romans 8.35

"I will tell of the LORD'S unfailing love; I will praise him for all he has done for us." Isaiah 63.7

Perhaps love is like the ocean
Full of conflict full of pain
Like a fire when it's cold outside
Thunder when it rains
If I should live forever
And all my dreams come true
My memories of love will be of you

"God has poured out his love into our hearts." Romans 5.5

And some say love is holding on
And some say letting go
And some say love is ev'rything
Some say they don't know

"The Spirit produces love, joy, peace . . ." Galatians 5.22

"These three remain: faith, hope, and love; and the greatest of these is love." 1 Corinthians 13.13

Perhaps love is like the ocean
Full of conflict full of pain
Like a fire when it's cold outside

Thunder when it rains
If I should live forever
And all my dreams come true
My memories of love will be of you

"This is how we know what love is: Christ gave his life for us." 1 John 3.16

"Keep yourselves in the love of God, as you wait for our Lord Jesus Christ in his mercy to give you eternal life." Jude 21

ACTIONS IN WORSHIP

If we are not careful, worship can easily become cerebral and dominated by too many words. Symbolic actions can be used to great effect, but they must be planned carefully and only used sparingly. Too frequent use of actions can appear gimmicky. Using actions in worship is not unlike the "symbolic actions" in some of the prophets. (See, for example, Ezekiel 3.1–3; 5.1–4). The following suggestions all work well, but it is better for a small group to work together on developing your own symbolic actions.

- Cut a number of "flames" from coloured paper — about 6" long and enough for each member of the group to have one. Prepare a "bush" from large twigs set in a pot. Each member writes the name of a person, or a particular concern for which they wish to pray on one of the "flames". One at a time, members fix their flame to the twigs, creating a colourful "burning bush". Either they read out the concern as they affix the flame, or the leader reads them when all have been added.
- Worship can begin by people gathering in darkness, and each being given a candle. One candle is lit, and then members pass the light from candle to candle until all are lit. This can be accompanied by sentences from scripture, or by quiet singing.
- A collection of flowers and greenery (either fresh or dried) is laid out, with one or more vases. At a suitable point in the worship, members are invited to add a piece to an arrangement, symbolizing the complementarity of Christians who worship together.

- A number of candles can be set in a large stand or sand tray in the centre of the room. As a person prays for a particular concern, she can light one of the candles.
- Ask members to come to the worship with a small stone. Either on arrival, or at some point in the service, the stones can be built into a cairn. This can be accompanied by reading a verse of scripture as each stone is added.

STRUCTURES FOR WORSHIP

Some groups will prefer informal, impromptu worship. Others will wish to use their familiar liturgies. Clearly, it would be a mistake to impose upon a group a totally unfamiliar way of worshipping — they would only feel insecure, and probably irritated.

Most services need a structure — it is very rare that a totally unstructured act of worship is successful. Those responsible for devising the worship will want to discuss what structures are appropriate. The introduction to *Patterns for Worship* (Church House Publishing,1990) gives excellent guidelines on creativity and flexibility in worship without the sacrifice of structure and balance. Alan Dunstan's book *Special Services for Festivals and Occasions* (Kevin Mayhew, 1991) gives many examples of simple, effective structures.

Most acts of worship will contain some of the following elements:

- Bible reading
- Bible exposition
- Singing
- Confession
- Intercession
- Prayers of dedication
- Silence
- Actions

Do not feel bound to do things in the same way as in your home Church. The residential act of worship is a good time to be adventurous. For example, Bible readings can be done in a variety of ways. *The Dramatised Bible* (Marshall, Morgan and Scott and Bible Society) is an essential item in your box of resources for worship. Having a number of short verses grouped around a theme read by a variety of voices is also effective. This collection of readings is good as a starter to a reflective session. Each should be read by a different person, quietly, with silence between.

Isaiah 40.29–31
"He strengthens those who are weak and tired. Even those who are young grow weak; young men can fall exhausted. But those who trust in the Lord for help will find their strength renewed. They will rise on wings like eagles; they will run and not get weary; they will walk and not grow weak."

Isaiah 30.15
" . . . quietly trust in me. Then you will be strong and secure . . . "

Ecclesiastes 3.7
" . . . the time for silence and the time for talk . . . "

It can often be effective to use a familiar and traditional part of worship in a new form. The Song of Simeon (Luke 2.29–32) has been used in services since the earliest times. This translation by Jim Cotter, from his book *Prayer at Night*, is a good example:

Before and after the Nunc Dimmittis:
Alleluia. The Holy Spirit will teach you all things, alleluia. And will guide you into all truth, alleluia, alleluia.

Nunc Dimmittis
Praise be to God, I have lived to see this day. God's promise is fulfilled, and my duty done.

At last you have given me peace, for I have seen with my own eyes, the salvation you have prepared for all nations — a light to the world in its darkness, and the glory of your people Israel.

Glory be to God, sustaining, redeeming, sanctifying, as in the beginning, so now, and for ever. Amen

(from *Prayer at Night: A Book for the Darkness* by Jim Cotter, Cairns Publications, 1983).

The Covenant Service from the Methodist Service Book can be used in its entirety, or adapted, for use at the end of a retreat or conference, as an act of dedication and commitment. At the heart of that service is the act of Covenant first used by John Wesley in 1755, and this can be utilized in a number of worship settings.

Lord God, Holy Father, since you have called us through Christ to share in this gracious Covenant, we take upon ourselves with joy the yoke of obedience and, for love of you, engage ourselves to seek and do your perfect will. We are no longer our own but yours.

I am no longer my own, but yours. Put me to what you will, rank me with whom you will; put me to doing, put me to suffering; let me be employed for you or laid aside for you, exalted for you or brought low for you; let me be full, let me be empty; let me have all things, let me have nothing; I freely and wholeheartedly yield all things to your pleasure and disposal. And now, glorious and blessed God, Father, Son and Holy Spirit, you are mine and I am yours. So be it. And the covenant now made on earth, let it be ratified in heaven. Amen.

If you are looking for ready–made services which are suitable for a wide range of traditions and are easy to adapt, the Taizé Office Book *Praise in all our Days,* although out of print, but still widely found in many retreat centres, is excellent. It can, of course, be effectively used with music from Taizé. The following service is a typical example.

A SHORT EVENING PRAYER

Introduction

Blessed be our God at all times,
now and always and for ever and ever:
Amen.

Come let us fall down and worship Christ among us, our King and our God.

God, holy; God, strong and holy; God, holy and immortal: have pity on us.

Psalm

Reading from Scripture

Responses

Heal my soul, for I have sinned against you.
Heal my soul, for I have sinned against you.

Have pity on me Lord,
For I have sinned against you.

Glory to the Father, and the Son, and the Holy Spirit.
Heal my soul, for I have sinned against you.

Silence

Hymn

Intercession

For the universal Church, that God give her everywhere peace
and unity, perseverance in her faith and mission, let us pray to
the Lord:
O Lord, hear our prayer.

For the whole people of God, that each one may be a servant of
Christ truly and faithfully, let us pray to the Lord:
O Lord, hear our prayer.

For those who are drawing near to the light of faith, that the
Lord guide their steps into the communion of the Body of
Christ, let us pray to the Lord:
O Lord, hear our prayer.

For all people, for those who are lonely, sick, hungry,
persecuted, let us pray to the Lord:
O Lord, hear our prayer.

Free Prayer

Collect

Almighty God, your glory was manifested in the Cross of our Lord Jesus Christ. May the contemplation of this love fill us with joy and hope, for he lives and reigns now and for ever.

Blessing

Let us bless the Lord,
We give our thanks to God.

May the God of all grace, who has called us to his eternal glory in Christ, after we have suffered for a while, make us perfect, confirm and strengthen us. To him be the power for ever and ever.
Amen.

Often you can take a single long prayer or reading as the basis for an act of worship, and simply add one or two elements to create a short service. An evening meditation taken from *A Way for the Pilgrim: A Book of Meditations* by J. Barrie Shepherd, (Saint Andrew Press 1991), forms an effective centre–piece.

Play a recording of Vaughan Williams' The Lark Ascending while members gather.

Bible Reading: Mark 14.32–42

Silence

Harden not your hearts

Worship with a soft heart
is no easy matter; there are so many factors,
influences which tend toward a stubborn
and unyielding attitude of hardness.

There are distractions which draw my thoughts
away from listening for God's inner voice:
petty little complaints about surroundings,
the temperature, the flower arrangements,
the choice of hymns, behaviour of my neighbours,
or their children in the pews.
On the other hand I get so caught up
in the beauty of the music, the glowing splendour
of stained glass, the literary elegance of prayers,
scripture readings, even the eloquent delivery
of the preacher, that I never hear the living word,
never notice the hand knocking at
the tight–shut door of my soul.

Beyond distractions are defences,
deliberate and devious ways in which I seek
to prevent myself from getting too involved,
from being reached and moved to action
by the message that I hear. Over the years
I have perfected these techniques until
they are almost automatic, subliminal.
I hear about the suffering of the hungry
and remind myself I sent a cheque last Christmas.
Corruption and injustice, the problems
of pollution, are all countered by
'What can one person do?'
As for the call to personal morality,
to responsibility and honesty and faithfulness,
I tend to wallow in my guilt rather than seeking
ways for the divine transforming grace to work
its miracles upon my life.

In the silence of this evening hour,
restore my listening ear.
Remind me of the joy of salvation,
the shining hope and vision in which I once began
this pilgrimage of faith. Then speak to me
your tender word that comforts and renews.
Soften my heart, O Lord, that it might yield
again to your bright, saving grace.

Amen

Song: O Lord, Hear My Prayer (Taizé)

BOOKS

There are, of course, large numbers of books of prayers and services available, and each Church will have its own traditions. Do not neglect the official service books of the different denominations. You can often find fresh and unfamiliar material in another Church's book, or even sometimes in your own! The following is a brief selection of books which I have found especially useful.

Worshipping Together, (Saint Andrew Press, 1991). This contains six complete orders of service, practical guidelines, and additional prayers. Particularly useful for non–eucharistic worship.

Prayer in the Morning, Prayer in the Day, Prayer at Night, by Jim Cotter, (Cairns Publications, 1983–1989). This series of books is based on a re–casting of the ancient offices of the Church and on Cotter's own translations of the Psalms. This material is not to everyone's taste, especially in the regular use of feminine images of God. These books are, however, stimulating works and contain a wealth of useable material for reflective worship.

A Way for the Pilgrim — A book of meditations by J. Barrie Shepherd, (Saint Andrew Press, 1991). A collection of meditations on passages of scripture specifically leading up to Easter, but useable throughout the year. For a short, quiet end to the day, a piece of music, a Bible reading and one of these meditations made an excellent act of worship.

Let All the World, (U.S.P.G., 1990), is a collection of liturgies, litanies and prayers from around the world. It contains material, including songs, from many traditions and cultures, and many of the complete services in it are suitable. Much of the material is unusual, and it readily lends itself to use by a number of voices.

The Easter Spirit compiled by Robert Van de Weyer and Pat Saunders, (Darton, Longman and Todd, 1990), is an anthology of readings and prayers. As the title suggests, the material is particularly suitable for the Easter season, but it can be used at any time. It is especially useful for groups compiling meditative acts of worship, perhaps of readings interspersed with recorded music.

The Iona Community Worship Book, (Wild Goose Publications, 1988), contains not only morning and evening worship and communion liturgies, but also services for justice, healing, peace, etc. (The wild goose is a Celtic symbol of the Holy Spirit.)

MUSIC

Every Church and group will have its own traditional and favourite books of hymns and songs, so there is little use in providing a list. The following are, however, particularly suitable because they are easy to sing and can be learned quickly. They sound good with a small group of instruments providing the accompaniment.

Wild Goose Songs (3 volumes) from the Iona Community. These are new to many people, and contain many catchy tunes.

Music from Taizé (2 volumes) published by Collins Liturgical.

A WEEKEND OF REFLECTION

This weekend combines a number of different approaches to spiritual reflection. Its purpose is to give participants a structure within which to use their time, while allowing them enough freedom to pursue their own paths. Within the weekend there are ideas taken from journaling, Ignatian reflection, and different methods of meditating on scripture and nature.

When planning a weekend such as this, the leaders must be aware of the need for space and time and quietness. Beware of trying to cram too much into the event. In some sessions, there should be very little talking: the task of the leaders is to provide an atmosphere within which prayer and reflection may take place. Silence will arise naturally at various points, but there is no need to impose it. Some people are comfortable with silence; others find it awkward and embarrassing. When the notes suggest a period of quiet, do not be worried if some people wish to talk — simply make it clear at the outset that some may wish to be quiet and that they should be allowed the opportunity.

At some points in the sessions, it is suggested that people should share in pairs or in small groups. Again, do not be rigid or heavily directive. Allow people to talk with those with whom they feel comfortable. If they prefer not to share their thoughts, do not try to compel them. In fact, if you have set the right atmosphere, most participants will want to share their reflections.

Deep feelings will almost certainly be provoked on a weekend such as this. Be ready to deal with them. It would be advisable for one of the leaders, or some other experienced person, to be available for counselling or spiritual guidance. It may be possible to give set times and places for this, or a simple announcement at the beginning that any of the leaders may approached might be sufficient.

Don't worry if some people want to use the time in ways other than you suggest. They may come with different needs, or simply find some of the methods of prayer uncongenial. As long as they do not disrupt the other members, allow them to use the weekend in their own way.

PROGRAMME

Friday

6.30 p.m.	Arrive
7.00 p.m.	Dinner
8.00 p.m.	Session I: Reflecting on my past.
9.30 p.m.	Worship

Saturday

8.00 a.m.	Worship
8.30 a.m.	Breakfast
9.30 a.m.	Session II: God's place in my past — Psalm 91
11.00 a.m.	Coffee
11.30 a.m.	Session III: God's place in my present — Psalm 23
1.00 p.m.	Lunch
Free afternoon	
4.00 p.m.	Tea
4.30 p.m.	Session IV: A Prayer Walk
6.30 p.m.	Dinner
8.00 p.m.	Session V: The Good Shepherd
9.30 p.m.	Worship

Sunday

8.30 a.m.	Breakfast
9.30 a.m.	Session VI: What have we learned? Preparing for worship
11.00 a.m.	Coffee
11.30 a.m.	Worship
1.00 a.m.	Lunch and departure

SESSION I: REFLECTING ON MY PAST

One of the most distinctive things about the Bible is the way the past is dealt with. To describe Christianity as a historical religion is true, but one must say much more about the way the Bible and the Church handle history. The claim that faith is based on history is not as straightforward as it seems. Imagine that a video camera had captured the events of the crossing of the Red Sea, or of Jesus's appearance to Mary in the garden. Would a person watching the video be compelled into faith? The answer is clearly "No"!

What we see in the Bible and in the life of the Church is a continual reflection on history. Past and present are re-assessed in the light of each other, and are allowed to play upon one another. In the light of the present, new questions are asked of the past; and in the light of the past, the present is challenged. The prophets call the people back to the covenant made with them by God; but they also gain a new understanding of the significance and meaning of the covenant as they face the challenges of contemporary living.

Israel and the Church found a number of major turning points in their history. For Israel the significant events were the Exodus; the reign of David and the building of the Temple; the fall of Jerusalem in 585BC; the exile and restoration. These historical turning points became the raw material which enabled them to see God at work in their history. For the Christian Church the events of the cross and resurrection; pentecost; the persecution of the early Christians; the conversion of the Roman Empire; and the Reformation provide similar material. The fact that different people might wish to have a different list of significant events is worth reflection.

We allow these turning points of history to act as critiques of our own present, and indeed to define us as people and as Christians. Thus, the tradition within which we stand will determine which turning points we take as important. The Reformation, the Oxford Movement, the Evangelical Revival, the birth of feminist theology — how we place ourselves in relation to these portrays to others and to ourselves much of what we are.

But this use of the past does not only apply to us as a Christian community. It also applies to us as individuals. During this weekend, I am inviting you to explore your own past; to allow it to criticize your present; and to re-assess your past in the light of what God is doing with you now.

We begin by reviewing the main turning points of our lives. I want you to spend about half an hour identifying the major events of your life — marriage, a change of job, the arrival of children, the death of a parent.

The turning points may have been planned and considered; they may have been accidental or coincidental.

Do not try too hard tonight to identify God's guidance in these events. Simply ponder your own past, and list the events.

When you have done that, find two or three other people, and tell each other about these turning points.

SESSION II — GOD'S PLACE IN MY PAST: PSALM 91

Read Psalm 91

Last night we thought about significant turning points in our lives. Some of those we will already have identified as times when God was guiding and supporting. Other events may have been difficult and painful, and it may not be at all clear whether God was in them.

During this session, I want you to concentrate on a single event during which you now see that God was leading you. This may not have been apparent at the time. It may be that only years later did you become aware that he was with you in this event. Choose an event which you can comfortably share with another person.

Take time to recreate this event in your own memory. Recall the circumstances, the other people involved. Remember the smells or colours; the words used by you and other people. Try to recreate in yourself the feelings which surrounded the event. Think about what God was saying to you at the time of this event; and think about what he is saying to you now through it. If you wish, read Psalm 91 again, and ask God to show you his care in the light of this Psalm.

Then try to symbolize how God was with you in this event. You might want to draw a picture; to choose a passage of scripture or a piece of poetry or the verse of a hymn.

When you have done this, find another person, and take 15–20 minutes each to share whatever you wish to share about this reflection.

SESSION III — GOD'S PLACE IN MY PRESENT: PSALM 23

Read Psalm 23

It is much harder to identify God's action in the uncertainty of the present than it is to see him at work in the past. The first step is to look at those parts of our present lives for which we are seeking his guidance.

Take about 20 minutes for the next section.

Using the imagery of Psalm 23, try to describe in your life:
"fields of green grass . . . quiet pools of fresh water" (verse 2)
the things which "give me new strength". (verse 3)
"the right paths" (verse 3) in which God is guiding you
"the deepest darkness" (verse 4)

You may then choose to do one or more of the following. It is unlikely that you will be able to do them all in the time given.

List the things in your present life which you would like to thank God for.

List the things you wish to ask God's forgiveness for.

List any areas of your life from which you feel God to be absent.

List things about which you are deeply concerned, and which you would like God to transform.

When you have made a list, offer it to God. Your offering may be an acted symbol — placing it on the altar in the chapel; lifting it up to the sky; speaking it aloud in prayer.

SESSION IV — A PRAYER WALK

Creation can lead us to the Creator and often we can hear God speaking through his created world if we will but be open and attentive to listen. Jesus reflected often on his Father's world and included these insights in his teaching (e.g. the birds of the air, the lilies of the field, the fig tree, and the chicks).

Here is a simple prayer exercise whereby we deliberately slow down and open ourselves to God. Leave about thirty minutes for the actual walk.

Go for a walk alone, deliberately slowing your pace. Take a few deep breaths. Now open yourself to God, asking him to speak to you either concerning a specific question or concern you may have or about something he wants to show you. Keep open to the outside world rather than simply mulling things over in your mind. Use your senses to become aware of what is going on around you. Use your eyes to look at things close up and at a distance. Become aware of shapes, colours, textures. Look at things in relation to each other. Does anything particularly attract your attention. If so, pause and take it in. Is God saying something through it?

Use your ears and really listen, both to sounds and to silence. Be aware of sounds going on inside yourself — hear your inner self but then move out again.

Use touch to become aware of different textures — the bark of a tree, the earth, grass, a wall. Again, if something attracts you, pause and explore it. Become aware of anything God might be saying. You are want to bring something back you have picked up — a stone, a twig, etc.

For 20 minutes or so, share as you want in groups of four or five people.

This idea is taken from *What Works?* by Anne Long in *Can Spirituality be Taught?* J. Robson and D. Lonsdale (eds) ACATE and British Council of Churches.

SESSION V — THE GOOD SHEPHERD

This session borrows some of the imaginative approach of Ignatian spirituality. You might begin by using one of the stillness exercises from Chapter Ten describing methods of reflection.

On a table in the centre of the group, arrange some items evocative of the life of a shepherd. A crook, a pile of stones, some wool, etc. Play some music, and invite participants to be still, look at the objects, and listen.

Read John 10.1–14

Help participants to picture the scene described by Jesus in their imagination. Use the following as a guide. Allow gaps for silence between the phrases and sentences. The exercise may take up to twenty minutes. Do not hurry. Tell participants that after you have read the Bible passage for the second time, they have thirty minutes to think and pray. They may stay where they are; go to their room; go for a walk; go to the chapel.

Picture a flock of sheep on a hillside. Look at the sweep of the hills; the craggy rocks; the dangerous cliffs. See the stone walls; smell the soil and grass; hear the wind.

Look at the sheep, scattered across the landscape. See some in

small groups; some high on the hilltops. Hear them bleating —
some with a contented sound; others calling urgently for they are
lost and frightened.

Now you see a shepherd striding into view. Watch him as he
climbs the hill. Observe his clothes; the things he carries. See how
he approaches his sheep; listen as he calls to them.

Now the shepherd begins to round up the sheep. See his tender-
ness; his care for them. See how he looks at them. Watch as they
are brought together and herded into the sheepfold. Observe the
fold — the texture of the rocks which make the walls.

The shepherd sits at the entrance to the fold, and you hear him
speak:

"I am the gate for the sheep . . . Whoever comes in by me will
be saved; he will come in and go out and find pasture."

"I am the good shepherd who is willing to die for the sheep."

Then the shepherd turns to you, and addresses you by your
name. He asks why you are here. Tell him.

Now the shepherd asks what you want him to do for you. Tell
him what you want him to do, and await his rely.

Read John 10.1–14 again.

SESSION VI — WHAT HAVE WE LEARNED?

It is important that time should be spent in this last session giving
participants the opportunity of sharing some of the experiences
they have had during the weekend. They should be helped to find
ways of carrying forward what they have learned into their lives,
and of expressing to themselves and to others what has happened
to them.

You may choose one of the endings described in Chapter Nine.
Whether this is done as a large group, in pairs, or in groups of four
or five will depend on the leaders' perception of how easily people
can share.

Allow 45 minutes for this, leaving half this session for preparation for worship.

TWENTY–FOUR HOURS OF BIBLE STUDY

This short residential session takes two major related biblical themes — Creation and Redemption — and looks at a series of passages by using a variety of different methods. The outline suggested is especially suitable for use during the period before Easter, but can be used at any time of the year. This approach could be used to study almost any biblical theme.

Day 1	
1.00 p.m.	Lunch
2.15 p.m.	Opening prayers.
	Session 1 — God's Good Creation
4.00 p.m.	Tea
4.30 p.m.	Session II — And the snake said . . .
6.00 p.m.	Dinner
7.30 p.m.	Session III — The Cross of Jesus
9.00 p.m.	Worship
Day 2	
8.00 a.m.	Worship
8.30 a.m.	Breakfast
9.30 a.m.	Session IV — A New Creation
11.00 a.m.	Coffee
11.30 a.m.	Session V — All things are brought back to God in him
1.00 p.m.	Lunch

SESSION I — GOD'S GOOD CREATION

Begin with a few minutes of opening prayer and, if the participants do not already know each other well, use one of the starters.

Genesis 1.1 — 2.4

This session aims to present the opening chapter of the Bible as a means of reflection, without intellectual study or discussion. The method suggested entails a considerable amount of preparation.

In the weeks preceding the event, gather together a collection of slides which illustrate the Genesis passage. Aim to have at least five or six slides illustrating each of the seven days of creation. Choose a piece or pieces of music, either to suit the whole presentation, or to fit each of the days. A reader should carefully rehearse with the slides and the taped music, so that the appropriate verses are read to the background of music, while the slides are projected.

Aim for a presentation lasting about 20 minutes. After this, suggest to participants that they do not discuss what they have seen or heard, but take the time remaining until tea to consider in silence God's goodness in creation, and the beauty of what he has made. If the weather is good, and the surroundings amenable, they may wish to do this outside.

SESSION II — AND THE SNAKE SAID . . .

Genesis 3.1–19

There is endless scope for using the Bible dramatically. This exercise is a role–play in which members of the group try to enter imaginatively into the story of the fall.

Arrange for the passage to be read by five people — a narrator, and people reading the parts of the snake, Adam, Eve and God. After the reading, divide into four equal groups, representing the four characters in the story. Each group should try to describe how it feels about the events of the story, while in the role of the particular character. What does it feel like to be Adam or Eve or God or the snake as the events happen, and how does it feel at the end of the story? Tell the groups that at the end of 30 minutes you want them, representing their character in the story, to have something to say to each of the other characters.

Begin the plenary session by asking each group in turn to say how they felt about their part in the events, and how they feel at the end of the story. Then invite each of them to say something to each of the other groups — first let the group representing Adam speak to the other groups, and let "God" speak last. Try to ensure that as far as possible the groups remain "in role", although it is likely that there will be a fair amount of humour. In the final 20 minutes, ask members to return to being themselves, and as a group reflect on what this exercise has brought to light about the passage.

SESSION III — THE CROSS OF JESUS

Mark 15.21–39

For this session, try an Ignatian–style reflection on the passage. Invite participants to relax (use one of the exercises from Chapter Ten on relaxation methods), then have the passage read very slowly, twice.

The following text is only one way of helping participants reflect on the story — use your own words if you are happier. Most importantly, allow lots of silence between the sentences and phrases, and try to make the reflection to last about twenty minutes.

Ask members to imagine themselves observing the scene.

"Feel the heat of the sun; smell the crowd; hear the noises of a large gathering of people baying for blood. Now become a character in the scene. You may be Simon of Cyrene, or one of the disciples, or a soldier, or a Pharisee. Think of how you feel as you observe what is happening. Watch as the nails are driven into Jesus' hands, and the cross is hauled into place. Hear the gasp of the crowd, and listen to the remarks people make.

Read the sign giving the reason for his execution: "The King of the Jews". Now listen to the mocking of the crowd: "He saved others, but he cannot save himself! Let us see the Messiah, the king of Israel, come down from the cross now, and we will believe in him"!

Suddenly, the sky is dark. What do you feel in the darkness? What do others in the crowd say about it? The darkness goes on and on — how do you feel after two or three hours of dark in the middle of the day? Then, for the first time, you hear Jesus speak. "My God, my God, why did you abandon me"? What do you think he means? Are you puzzled? Do you understand? Then, "with a loud cry Jesus died". How do you feel? Listen to the soldier say, "This man was really the Son of God". Do you agree? If the soldier is right, how does it affect you? You turn away and leave the scene. What are you going to do now? Speak to God about what you must do as a result of what you have seen and heard.

Read the passage again, and allow about 15 minutes silence.

Then in smaller groups, ask participants to discuss how they react to the exercise. They may like to share some of the things they felt and prayed, but do not force this.

SESSION IV — A NEW CREATION

John 20.19–29
This session is more open than the others, and tries to relate episodes in participants' own pilgrimages of faith to these two gospel occurrences. The passage contains two stories about the risen Jesus appearing to his disciples — the breathing of the Spirit, and the doubts and faith of Thomas.

Divide into small groups of about four, and invite participants to tell stories from their own experience which they feel illuminate for them the gospel passage.

John 20.19–23 might provoke stories about the peace given by Jesus; about the receiving of the Spirit; or about experiences of giving and receiving forgiveness.

John 20.24–29 may encourage stores about doubts and difficulties in the past of the present; and stories about faith and belief.

Allow participants to tell these stories at some length, and suggest that the other members of the group question them about their experiences and how they see them to be related to these specific passages.

SESSION V — ALL THINGS ARE BROUGHT BACK TO GOD IN HIM

Colossians 1.15–20
Ephesians 1.15–23
Working in groups of five or six people, read the passages slowly, and then answer the following questions:

1. What might it mean that "Christ rules there above all heavenly rulers, authorities, powers, and lords; he has a title superior to all titles of authority in this world and in the next."? (Ephesians 1.21) What are the implications of this for politics; for our secular occupations; for ethics; for the media, etc.?
2. Colossians 1.22–23 links Christ's lordship over all things directly with the Church. What implications do these passages have for our understanding of the Church?

3. "God made peace through his Son's sacrificial death on the cross and so brought back to himself all things, both on earth and in heaven." (Colossians 1.20) What does this mean? How does it affect our view of God's creation now?

Allow the groups to work for about 1 hour, and then reconvene and finish before lunch with one of the endings suggested in Chapter Nine.

A CHURCH CONFERENCE

Many congregations of all denominations are discovering the value of a weekend away together to look at the purpose of their Church and to give concentrated thought to the way it might develop. Some Churches find this a useful exercise to undertake with the Church Council or other leadership group, while some issue an open invitation to any members of the Church who may be interested. The outline suggested below is flexible, and can be easily altered to include other main topics.

It is essential to set a tone different from that of the Church's ordinary business meetings. The residential event should contain time for worship and reflection, and for informal talking and relaxation. It is a good opportunity to extend the amount of participation in worship — people will often take part in the leadership of worship during a weekend such as this even if they firmly refuse to do so in their home Church.

PROGRAMME

Friday

6.30 p.m.	Arrive
7.00 p.m.	Dinner
8.00 p.m.	Session I — The purpose of the Church
9.30 p.m.	Worship

Saturday

8.00 a.m.	Worship
8.30 a.m.	Breakfast
9.30 a.m.	Session II — The Church's worship
11.00 a.m.	Coffee
11.30 a.m.	Session III — Church and community
1.00 p.m.	Lunch

Free afternoon	
4.00 p.m.	Tea
4.30 p.m.	Session IV — The way ahead
6.30 p.m.	Dinner
8.00 p.m.	Session V — Spiritual Reflection
9.30 p.m.	Worship
Sunday	
8.30 a.m.	Breakfast
9.30 a.m.	Session VI — Conclusion and Preparation for worship
11.00 a.m.	Coffee
11.30 a.m.	Worship
1.00 p.m.	Lunch and Departure

SESSION I — THE PURPOSE OF THE CHURCH

This session should contain some input as a framework around which members can think, and plenty of time for small group discussion. If the group do not already know one another well, use one of the "starters" from Chapter Seven.

The opening input may be along the lines of the following — it gives enough to think about without constraining thought. It could be delivered as a talk, suitably amended to fit the context, or it could be photocopied and given to participants to read in advance. Brief discussion in the whole group should be followed by members answering the question sheet individually, and then sharing their answers in small groups of four to six people. The groups' conclusions can be written up on large sheets of paper and hung on the wall — hopefully acting as a discussion starter during free time.

What is the Church?

There have been many ways of understanding the Church in Christian History. It has been viewed as an *institution* founded by

Jesus with the primary task of being a channel of grace and teaching. The role of the hierarchy is to ensure that the teaching is in accordance with tradition, and the role of laity is passive acceptance.' Secondly, the Church may be described as a mystical communion, *the body of Christ.* Its function is to help members to achieve union with God, which is brought about through fellowship with one another in Christ. Thirdly the Church has been portrayed as the *servant of the world,* drawing on the picture of Jesus washing the disciples' feet at the last supper. According to this model the Church is to serve the community in which it is located and is to be outward looking. Fourthly, the Church is the *sacrament* of God's presence in the world. "As the soul is in the body, so the Church is in the world", says an anonymous second century epistle. The fifth model is of the Church as *herald.* Its task is to proclaim the good news, and wherever the gospel of Christ is being proclaimed, there is the authentic Church.

Each of these models has its strengths and weaknesses, and they must be allowed to inform and criticize each other, for reliance on one model to the exclusion of the others leads to a distorted view of the nature of the Church. A Church community which sees itself only as the world's servant, and forgets the herald model, becomes indistinguishable from a social services department. A Church which takes note only of the body of Christ model is liable to stress the importance of membership boundaries and of internal fellowship, and to ignore other aspects. It is interesting to note that the predominant model of the Church used in the Anglican Alternative Service Book (ASB) and in the Methodist Service Book is that of the body of Christ, and it is worth speculating on the effect this has on the those Churches's understanding of themselves at present.

While the list of five major models described above probably gives an accurate picture of the way the Church has been understood historically, there are a large number of other models of the Church in current usage. Probably the most prevalent is the Church as family. Family services proliferate; many Christians, lay and ordained, refer to the Church as the family of God; the baptism service in the ASB contains the greeting, "we welcome you into the Lord's family". This development must find echoes in people's experience for it to have become so popular, but it is not without its drawbacks. The contemporary nuclear family has no biblical precedent, and although there are almost a hundred images or models of the Church in the New Testament, not one of them is family. The writers talk of the household of God — meaning a three generation family together with servants and workers — but never of family. This, taken together with the broken state of much family life in our society, must make us careful of using this one model of the Church to the exclusion of others.

One model which has recently been rehabilitated is of the Church as a place of healing. The suspicion of the miraculous which came with rationalism and the growth of modern science spilled over into the Churches so that to expect, or to pray for, miracles has been regarded as slightly eccentric for most of this century. It is good that a new awareness of this aspect of the gospel has arisen, and that spiritual, mental and physical wholeness are now high on the list of priorities for many Churches.

Some Churches view their main task as teaching, and seem to major on the idea of a Church as a school or college. They have a body of information — the gospel and tradition — to hand on, and they run highly organized teaching schemes for children and adults, and teaching often takes place in house groups. Until recently British Churches did not use this model extensively, and in this country the Roman Catholic Church has successfully delegated the responsibility for teaching children to its schools. Churches in the USA, where Sunday morning often means not only attendance at worship, but also an adult Bible class, use this model in large measure.

The Church as a "worship society" may not be obvious as a candidate for a model, but in fact many Churches see this as their main purpose. To be able to escape from the stresses of everyday life into timeless worship offered with dignity is a reason often given by people for choosing a particular Church. Worship, and sometimes the care of the building in which the worship is set, become the primary goals of the congregation, and the clergy in these Churches spend the majority of their time preparing for and leading worship.

The Church as the guardian of society's morals is a common model, and is frequently heard on the lips of politicians and parents of schoolchildren. Its function is thought to be to help educate the nation's children into their duty towards the community, and to ensure that all citizens take their responsibilities seriously. The importance of teaching the ten commandments is usually stressed by those who espouse this model.

For some people, although only rarely for whole congregations, the dominant model of the Church is as a "conservative association". It is the body, and the place, where the last defences against an ever–encroaching, distasteful, modern world are erected. Change in morality, in worship, in the Church buildings, in the structure of society, are all vehemently opposed from the pulpit and in the pews.

Other models could be suggested — the Church as insurance company, just in case there is a God; the Church as a place for society's misfits; the Church as a social agency — although these models are usually found only in small pockets.

It is most unusual to find any of the models described above used in isolation. Any Church usually sees itself as a mixture of models, and although one may predominate over a period of time, others will be used. Sometimes the dominant model will be replaced with another for a short time — for example during a mission or stewardship campaign. A model may be discarded, perhaps with a change of minister. Thus a Church may view itself as a worshipping community, while laying emphasis on teaching. Or it may take the servant model as dominant, while laying stress on the importance of internal fellowship.

QUESTION SHEET — TO BE ANSWERED INDIVIDUALLY THEN SHARED IN GROUPS.

Which of the following models or descriptions of the Church do you find reflect your understanding of the Church most accurately? Indicate which you feel to be the three most important descriptions.

☐ The Church is a teaching institution which instructs people in religious truth.

☐ The Church is a place of healing for those who are hurting spiritually.

☐ The Church is the fellowship of God's faithful people.

☐ The Church is a place for religious people to express their private feelings.

☐ The Church is the body entrusted by Jesus to proclaim the good news.

☐ The Church is the servant of the community — it exists primarily to benefit those who are outside it.

☐ The Church is the scene of a struggle between God and the devil.

☐ The Church is the method used by God to bring his Kingdom into being.

☐ The Church is the preserver of moral rights and wrongs in society.

☐ The Church is the means by which Christ is present in the world.

☐ The Church is a place where you can escape from the pressures of the world.

☐ The Church is a place to go to for the most important events in your life, such as baptisms, weddings and funerals.

☐ The Church is God's way of changing the world.

☐ The Church is the way God offers sacraments to people.

☐ The Church is the place to go to for occasions of national importance such as Remembrance Sunday or a royal wedding.

SESSION II — THE CHURCH'S WORSHIP

This session has two related aims. The first is to produce a realistic assessment of the present state of worship in your Church; the second is to agree on some aims for the direction in which the worship might develop.

1. Allow about 30 minutes for this exercise. On large sheets of paper, produce an outline of the Church's present pattern of worship. This should be done as a "brainstorm" session, with participants calling out their points. Begin by making a skeleton with times and types of services, and then on separate sheets list the main factors in each of the services. Try to reach a consensus that this description is an accurate reflection of the Church's worship. This method will work for up to about fifteen people. If there are more than this, you will probably need to divide into two groups.

2. Divide into groups of about six. Ask the groups to answer the following two questions, and to produce wall charts giving their findings:

- What needs in the Church or the community are not being met in the present pattern of worship?
- How might we adjust the pattern to meet these needs?

Stick the sheets on the wall, where they can be read during coffee.

SESSION III — CHURCH AND COMMUNITY

This session aims to take a realistic look at how the Church is involved in the community, and to produce some aims for future work.

1. Ask individuals to draw a picture illustrating some of the ways the Church is involved in the local community. The example might give participants some ideas. If it helps, photocopy the diagram on to an overhead projector slide and show it as a discussion starter.
2. Have a large map of the parish or area served by the Church prepared. Mark on it the main centre of gathering and social provision, e.g. schools, employers, places of leisure, old people's clubs, pubs, playgroups, etc. Ask participants to mark on the map anything which has been omitted.

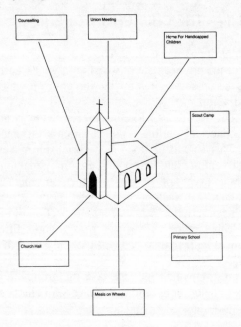

3. In groups of about six, ask members to answer two questions:
   - Who is not provided for in the community? Answers might be, for example, single mothers, those sleeping rough at night.
   - Where in the community is the Church not present? Referring to the drawings made earlier will help — the Church as an institution and as its individual members may be present in a surprisingly large number of places.
4. Report these findings back to the whole group, and agree on one or two aims for the Church's future involvement in the community. These can include working with institutions, such as schools, or individuals, e.g. homeless people.

SESSION IV — THE WAY AHEAD

The purpose of this session is to produce some specific plans in various areas of the Church's life. The plans should be attainable and limited; it is much better to plan to introduce a new hymn book than to aim to improve the quality of worship. You know when you have achieved the first, but have no way of assessing when you have reached the latter. Plans should also be timed — we will do this by the end of next year — and there should be some indication of who will be responsible for ensuring that they are carried out.

1. Prepare a large chart with headings relating to the areas of Church life which you want to plan for. This is probably best done in advance by the planning group, but should leave some space for ideas which emerge at the conference. Under each of the headings, mark columns for the time scale you wish to plan. Headings might include: worship, finance, property, children and youth, mission, Church and community, etc.
2. Divide into small groups, each of which will do the detailed planning for one heading. If the Church already has a committee system, it is probably desirable that the groups should consist largely, but not exclusively, of the relevant committee members. If there is no committee system, try to ensure that those with interest and expertise in a certain area work in that group. Groups should produce no more than two aims under each year.

The results of each group's deliberations should be displayed ready for discussion in Sunday morning's session.

SESSION V — REFLECTION

Choose one of the reflective sessions from the worship section, or from the weekend of reflection.

SESSION VI — CONCLUSIONS

Allow each group a maximum of 5 minutes to present their plans. Give time to discuss whether the plans presented accurately reflect the mind of the Church, and decide together which plans should be presented to the Church Council or other decision making body at its next meeting with a request for implementation.

Use one of the endings from Chapter Nine.

STORY, HISTORY, AND FAITH

This residential session is deliberately slightly more "intellectual" than some of the other examples. It could be used with a group of adults preparing for full membership of the Church, or for a group asking for an interesting and stretching approach to their faith. The introductions to the sessions are brief outlines. They can be expanded by the leadership, or they could be photocopied and given to participants, with one member being asked to introduce each session.

Ask participants to come prepared to tell a story, lasting up to 5 minutes. It can be taken from any source — a children's book, a novel, a real experience, the Bible. It should be a story which moves them, and which for them carries meaning.

Day 1	
3.30 p.m.	Arrive
4.00 p.m.	Tea
4.30 p.m.	Session I — The importance of stories
6.30 p.m.	Dinner
7.30 p.m.	Session II — Story and national identity
9.00 p.m.	Worship
Day 2	
8.30 a.m.	Breakfast
9.30 a.m.	Session III — The story of Jesus
11.00 a.m.	Coffee
11.30 a.m.	Worship
1.00 p.m.	Lunch
2.00 p.m.	Session IV — The Church's story about itself

SESSION I — THE IMPORTANCE OF STORIES

Our culture has a fund of stories. Nursery rhymes and fairy stories help children to define and understand the world in which they live. *The Babes in the Wood, Snow White,* and so many others shape their understanding of family life and of the nature of society, and they help children to develop an outline morality. It is instructive to reflect on the brokenness and horror at the centre of many of these stories. Modern children's stories, such as those told by Roald Dahl and the Revd. W. Awdry continue in the same tradition, and provide material for children to interact with as they increase their awareness of adult society.

Nations also tell stories about themselves to define who and what they are. This is no comment on whether the stories are "true" or not — some contain more factual basis than others. Much history teaching is a nation's story about itself, and that is perhaps why the curriculum of that subject is always politically contentious. Remembrance Sunday is a particularly good example of the collective telling and enacting of a story about the defeat of evil, and an explanation of how so many friends and relatives of those alive today came to die. Shakespeare's history plays show how stories (which may bend the historical facts) were used to create national identity and purpose, and how drama may be used to validate the political status quo.

As individuals, we tell stories about ourselves. Often these stories are told to our children — about how mummy and daddy met; about what happened on holiday; about what children said and did when young. These stories have the power to define and describe the child's existence.

There is also a set of stories about God's interaction with humanity, both in the Scripture, and in other sources such as the Churches' history and the lives of individual Christians. This weekend we will try to discover how the many sets of stories we use — about ourselves, our morality and place in society, about our nation, about God and his Church — interact and enlighten each other.

Divide into groups of four, and ask each of the members to tell the story they have come prepared with to the others in the group.

Then ask them to discuss whether these stories could be translated into other terms — could the meaning, for example, be distilled into a statement, or a recommendation?

Conclude by asking the groups to discuss why stories play such an important part in shaping our self–understanding.

SESSION II — STORY AND NATIONAL IDENTITY

For an individual, one's personal history defines who one is. Not only is one shaped by genetic inheritance and upbringing, but also by the series of happenings and recurring rituals. These give a framework of memories which are reflected on, and cherished, or perhaps in some cases, suppressed. Events which are significant to the individual are linked to what happens in the world around — my outlook is deeply affected by the fact that my formative years were in the 1960s.

The same is true of human communities, especially in communities which are bound together by shared experiences. To be British is share a particular history. Interestingly, a Scot might want to put different historical events at the centre of the stage from those stressed by the English.

Perhaps the most distinctive feature of the Jewish people is their sense of history. Even now, they are bound together by a shared history which includes not only the Exodus and the exile, but also the pogroms, the holocaust and the founding of the State of Israel. Their sense of history goes back, however, to the beginning of human history.

From a secular viewpoint the history of Israel is no more unusual than the stories of many other small nations caught in the whirlpool of power politics. The strains of being on the borders of Egypt, Assyria and Babylon are not very different from the trials of Poland in the nineteenth and twentieth centuries. Most of the major biblical episodes relate directly to geography and politics. The migrations of people in the second millenium BC are reflected in the stories about Abraham, Joseph and Moses. The invasions by Assyria are seen reflected in much of the prophetic material.

In this sense, Israel is a minor sideshow in the history of the ancient Near East, and her cultural achievements are certainly overshadowed by those of her neighbours — nothing she produces compares with the glories of Greece and Egypt.

The difference is that for Israel, the story is also sacred history, because in her historical experiences the meaning of human life is disclosed in a unique way. The uniqueness of the Old Testament lies in the conviction that God is disclosing himself in this series of events. In the Scripture we do not have just a series of truths about

God, nor do we only have profound sayings and rules. We have the story of God's actions in the Jewish people — we have a saving history. God works out his purpose in the history of this people. So the Old Testament is at heart a narration of God's activity. In one sense all human history is the theatre of God's action, and all nature is his handiwork; but in Israel there is a historical drama which changes human perspectives, and has greatly affected the course of all human affairs.

When we tell our own history, we probably start with a series of significant events — our first memory, the death of a relative, starting school, moving house. Only later do we fill in our genealogy, the history of our parents, the more obscure periods. We select significant memories from the standpoint of the present. So it is with nations, and so it is with Israel. One crucial historical event created her as a self–conscious community. That event was so decisive, so formative, that all earlier happenings and all subsequent episodes were seen in its light. Even today, Jewish people regard the Exodus as the mainspring of their vocation and destiny. The Passover is not just a remembering; not just a "once upon a time". By telling the story and enacting the events of the first Passover, the believing Jew becomes a participant in the event, and the past enters into the present.

Split into groups of about six, and ask each group to look at *one* of the following passages, and then answer the question.

Exodus 12.1–12
Exodus 13.17–20
Exodus 14.15–31
Exodus 15

What does this passage say about God and his relationship with the people of Israel? Make a list of all the points which the group feels are made about God in this passage.

Write the views on large sheets of paper, and spend 20 minutes comparing the results.

SESSION III — THE STORY OF JESUS

Jesus of Nazareth was one of the great storytellers of history. Such was his use of language and the power of his observation of human relationships and nature that stories such as the Good Samaritan, the Prodigal Son and the Sower have become part of the culture of many societies.

But it is not only the stories told by Jesus that hold such power. The story about Jesus — his birth and life, death and resurrection — is supremely memorable and effective. And the difference between this story and all other stories is that Christians claim that the story of Jesus is not just historically true — it is a story which happened — but also that it is unique. There is no other story like it, not in the sense that there is no other story like Hamlet, but that no other story, whether historical or not, has the power to transform lives in the way the story of Jesus does.

There are a number of senses in which the story of Jesus is held to be true. First, it is a record of historical events. Christians might differ over the accuracy and relative importance of some of the historical detail in the gospel narratives, but almost all would agree that we have a reliable basic historical framework.

The story of Jesus is also "true to life"; it is recognized as an accurate description of what it is to be human, and of our relationship with God. These stories of and about Jesus awaken response in the reader and the hearer, by moving and challenging.

The moving, challenging nature of these stories is not easily translated into non–narrative terms. Historically the Christian community has wanted to describe Jesus in terms which it thought to be more permanent than stories — creeds, confessions, philosophical statements, etc. These doctrinal formulations are important, but they lack the power of the biblical stories to challenge — millions have become Christian after hearing the story of the cross and resurrection of Jesus; have any been converted by listening to the Nicene Creed or the Westminster Confession?

In groups, read the story of the Good Samaritan (Luke 10.25–37) and the Prodigal Son (Luke 15.11–32). Why do the stories of Jesus constitute such a strong challenge? Perhaps the groups would find it helpful to rewrite one of these stories in a contemporary setting.

How does the story about Jesus differ from the stories of Jesus? Read, for example, Mark 14.22–52.

SESSION IV — THE CHURCH'S STORY ABOUT ITSELF

St Augustine wrote his *Confessions* in 397–398, when he was 43 — ten years after his baptism and six years after his ordination as a

priest. The first nine volumes cover 33 years of Augustine's life —
from his birth to the death of his mother, Monica, in 387. It is an
attempt to come to terms with his personal history and identity by
means of the Christian faith, rather than the over zealous testimony
of the recent convert. *Confessions* operates on different levels — it
is both a series of episodes which tell a personal history, and a
series of interpretations of that history. The events selected by
Augustine seem to be prompted not by the intrinsic significance of
the events themselves, but for the way in which the events illuminate the train of interpretation.

By telling his story in this form, Augustine has had an enormous effect on how individuals interpret the development of their
own faith. It is possible to argue that most Christian autobiography
and testimony takes its framework from *Confessions*.

Another method of describing Christian meaning is the pattern
suggested in *Pilgrim's Progress*. In his fictional story, Bunyan
takes a common religious experience — pilgrimage — and applies
it to life, so that all experience becomes part of a journey. This is a
powerful symbol of the dynamic nature of the Christian faith, and
it is a deeply memorable method which has etched itself on to
Western Christian thought.

It seems that certain methods of story telling, certain frame-
works, and a particular series of events define particular Christian
communities, just as they define nations or individuals.

There are stories of journeys to freedom — the Pilgrim Fathers,
the Huguenots — which have close parallels with the Exodus
story.

There are stories of protest — Martin Luther, John Wesley,
George Fox — which challenge the Church to constant renewal.

There are stories of martyrdoms — St Alban, Thomas à Becket,
Martin Luther King — which place before us the importance of
fidelity to the faith whatever the cost.

There are stories of doctrinal disputes during the first four centuries of the Church's history and during the Reformation, which
tell of our search for truth.

Within the Christian community, different individuals and different traditions will select from among the available stories in
order to build up a picture of their own Christian identity. One
Church might value stories of sainthood and martyrdom, another
might focus on stories of protest and renewal.

The following exercise is a sort of "desert island discs", but
with Christian stories. Give participants about fifteen minutes to

make a list of their four favourite non–biblical Christian stories. Some may be true, such as the martyrdom of Becket; others may be fictional such as the Narnia Chronicles of C.S. Lewis. Then divide into groups of four, and ask each group to produce an agreed list of four stories. If members of the group are unfamiliar with the stories suggested by others, the person who suggests a story may outline it. Write the agreed list on large sheets of paper, and display it during a break.

A final hour could be given to drawing together these four sessions, and the event can finish with one of the "endings" suggested in Chapter Nine.

WOMEN, THE BIBLE, AND THE CHURCH

It has become increasingly common for groups of women to meet residentially and study Christian topics together. These groups range from a regular retreat for the Mothers' Union to gatherings of radical feminists. The range of material for such groups need not, of course, be any different from that offered to mixed or male groups, but the increasing awareness that women's and men's spiritual needs and experiences may be different have led to the development of special liturgies for women, books of prayer for women, and the publication of Bible studies for women.

The residential sessions suggested here try to take a middle line — they are not in the radical feminist tradition, but they do take seriously the distinctive position of women both in the Bible and in today's Church.

The material is taken from two sources, each of which is a course of study sessions, but can easily be adapted for residential use. *Women's Lives* is a series of eight study sessions written by Rosemary Dawson, and published by the British Council of Churches, 1987. Sessions I, II and IV are taken from that course. An excellent series of four Bible study courses has been published by Bible Society: *Women in the Church, Women in the World, Women at Home,* and *Women Alone?* Session III is from *Women in the World* by Jeni Parsons.

It is important to give careful consideration to worship for this residential, and the leadership team should discuss to what extent the services need to reflect women's distinctive experience. The books by Jim Cotter mentioned in Chapter Twelve on worship are especially appropriate.

Day 1	
11.00 a.m.	Coffee
11.30 a.m.	Session I — Women's portion
1.00 p.m.	Lunch
2.00 p.m.	Session II — Women and God

4.00 p.m.	Tea
4.30 p.m.	Session III — Women and work
6.30 p.m.	Dinner
8.00 p.m.	Meditation and preparation for tomorrow's worship
Day 2	
8.30 a.m.	Breakfast
9.30 a.m.	Session IV — Women and the Church
11.00 a.m.	Coffee
11.30 a.m.	Conclusions and worship
1.00 p.m.	Lunch

SESSION I — WOMEN'S PORTION

Luke 10.38–42 concerns the differing roles and perspectives of two women, Mary and Martha. Many women today are able to draw parallels between this story and their own experience.

This session does not require you to be budding actors. It asks you to put yourselves in the shoes of Mary, Martha and Jesus and to see the story through their eyes.

1. One woman reads Luke 10.38–42 to the rest of the group. Allow a few moments afterwards for some quiet reflection. Those who have done some preparatory work can share with the others what they have learnt about:
   — the social position of women in first century Palestine.
   — the author of the Gospel and his purposes in writing it.

   (15 minutes)

2. The group then splits into three sub–groups. Each sub–group takes the part of one of the characters in the story. Imagine what that person's viewpoint would be. Each person asks herself: "How am I (as Mary, Martha or Jesus) feeling?" "How am I feeling towards the other two characters?" "Why am I behaving as I am?" Share your feelings with other members of your sub–group. Speak in the first person. It is particularly important for those in the "Jesus" sub–group to speak in the first person

and to say what they would feel in this position. (15 minutes)

3. Form new groups with a Mary, Martha and a Jesus in each. With each person still in her role, hold a conversation which follows on from the incident described in Luke 10.38–42. Continue to speak in the first person. Share what you are feeling and respond to what is said to you. (15–20 minutes)

4. After the conversation, the groups come together again to consider the following questions:

   • Why was this an important story for Luke to include in his Gospel?

   • What new insights have struck you as a result of this exercise?

   • What is the meaning of the story for your life — and for the life of your Church?

   • "Don't be a Martha"! What would happen if nobody was?

Would you like to rewrite this Bible story? If so, do so!

SESSION II — WOMEN AND GOD

1. Draw a diagram or write down a few words which expresses what God is for you. If this difficult, remind yourself of a time when God seemed close by and go from there.

2. List the names and characteristics of God which you recall from the Bible or from hymns. Indicate which of these you find most helpful and true to your experience.

   Go through the list together. Write M by the names and characteristics which you think of as male and F by those that you think of as female. Write both where you associate the names and characteristics with neither sex.

   What picture of God emerges? Is it adequate? How does it compare with your experience of God as expressed in the first exercise?

3. Do the verses below feature in your list, or do they fill out the picture? Discuss your responses to them.

   "I will cry out like a woman in labour". (Isaiah 42.14)

   "I will comfort you in Jerusalem, as a mother comforts her child".

   (Isaiah 66.13)

   "Jerusalem, Jerusalem . . . How many times have I wanted to put my arms round all your people, just as a hen gathers her

chicks under her wings." (Matthew 23.37)
4. Consider the following perceptions of God and Jesus:

"And thou, Jesus, sweet Lord,
art thou not also a mother?
Truly, Thou art a mother,
the mother of all mothers,
who tasted death, in thy
desire to give life to thy children."
                    Anselm, Archbishop of Canterbury, 1093

"The mother can give her child to suck of her milk, but our
precious Mother Jesus can feed us himself, and does most
courteously and most tenderly with the blessed sacrament
which is the most precious food of life. And though our earthly
mother may suffer her children to perish, our heavenly mother,
Jesus, may never suffer us who are his children to perish, for he
is almighty, all wisdom and all love."
                    Julian of Norwich (14th Century)
                    Revelations of Divine Love
                    Chapters 60 and 61

How do these add to your understanding of God?
5. In pairs, write short prayers which take account of both your
   experiences as women and your experiences of God. Use these
   to close the session.

SESSION III — WOMEN AND WORK

This session aims to explore the experiences of women's work,
both waged and unwaged, and to reflect on attitudes in the Bible to
what is traditionally perceived as women's work.

Read Genesis 3.14–21 and Luke 10.38–42

The Genesis story describes the results of the disobedience of
Eve, Adam, and the snake in the garden. Each will have to struggle
not only with the others but also with his or her environment and
the future. The woman and the man will have to labour hard in
their different ways and live without equality and also without intimacy with God. (Genesis 3.23–24) There is a discussion about
roles in the story from Luke when Jesus meets Mary and Martha.
In five short verses the author captures a debate that will be famil-

iar to many people who experience the hard work of housekeeping and who struggle with priorities — in this case between caring for human, physical needs and hearing about the good news of the kingdom, where God will meet all needs.

Group activity

Ask each person to make a list of all the types of work she does.

1. In twos or threes share the lists of work, paid and unpaid, that you do. Then discuss the Genesis passage and its explanation of why women and men have to labour so hard.
2. In the main group talk about whether you could imagine a world without the hard work of childbirth, manual labour and intellectual effort.
3. Talk about where you see God involved in your own work.

Prayer

Pray for the women and men whose work is seemingly without reward or recognition, and who are broken by their labour. Pray for the strength to challenge the oppression that results. Pray together:

O God, the power of the powerless,
you have chosen as your witnesses
those whose voice is not heard.
Grant that, as women first announced
the Resurrection
though they were not believed,
we too may have courage
to persist in proclaiming your word.
In the power of Jesus Christ, Amen.

SESSION IV — WOMEN AND THE CHURCH

Case Study

1. One horrible day I woke up to the realisation that I was completely alone. I had worked my way through college and had

a good job. I've lived alone all my life since I left home.

There doesn't seem to be a place for me, even at church. Last Sunday one of the older women said to me, "We don't know what to do with you. You're too old for the young people's group and too young for the older person's group. And you're not married so we can't put you in the married group." Her words were like acid on my heart, and the way I feel now I'm never going to church again. I've tried to live a Christian life, and I've tried to cooperate and not be an oddball. But that is just what an unmarried women in the church is — an oddball.

Would you try and persuade this woman to come back to church?

What would you say?

What expectations, if any, does the church have of women as mothers, wives or single people?

How do you feel about these expectations?

2. "The church would fall apart without women". Would yours? Draw a diagram to show the activities of your church and who does what (men? women? both?). Put the activities you see as most important nearer the centre of the diagram. Show your diagrams to one another. Are your priorities the same as those of your church, or of others in the group? What is your contribution? Would you like to change it in any way?

3. Who for us men and for our salvation came down from heaven

Almighty God, our heavenly Father, we confess that we have sinned against you and against our fellow men

> Father of men in whom are one
> All humankind beneath the sun,
> 'Stablish the work in thee begun
>
> O Christ, our elder brother, who
> By serving man God's will did do
> Help us to serve our brethren too.
>
> The English Hymnal, No 528

Does this language bother you? For what reason do some people find it offensive whilst others resist alterations?

Finish with one of the endings from Chapter Nine.

CONCLUSION

Give it a try! Leading and taking part in residential events with a Church or group of Christians is an exciting and rewarding way to explore and deepen one's faith. It will be hard work and you will make mistakes, but the experiences and the memories of the times away will enrich the Christian life of many people — not least that of the leaders.

If you have not yourself been on a retreat or a Christian conference, do try to take part in one before attempting to lead. And remember the value of team work — gather together a group of people with enthusiasm and vision who can plan and organize the event.

The potential strength of stepping aside is enormous — if you are looking for ways to strengthen the life and fellowship of your Church, then this might be for you.